Learn
HTML
and CSS
with w3schools

Hege Refsnes, Ståle Refsnes, Kai Jim Refsnes,
Jan Egil Refsnes with C. Michael Woodward

WILEY
Wiley Publishing, Inc.

Learn HTML and CSS with w3schools

Published by
Wiley Publishing, Inc.
111 River Street
Hoboken, NJ 07030-5774
www.wiley.com

Copyright © 2010 by Wiley Publishing, Inc., Indianapolis, Indiana

Published simultaneously in Canada

ISBN: 978-0-470-61195-1

LOC/CIP: 2010924594

Manufactured in the United States of America

10 9 8 7 6 5 4 3 2 1

w3schools Authors/Editors

w3schools' mission is to publish well-organized and easy-to-understand online tutorials based on the W3C Web standards.

Hege Refsnes

Hege is a writer and editor for w3schools. She works to improve the usability and accessibility of the Web.

Hege has been writing tutorials for w3schools since 1998.

Ståle Refsnes

Ståle has ten years of Internet development experience, developing all the Web-based solutions for The Norwegian Handball Federation.

Ståle has been writing tutorials for w3schools since 1999.

Kai Jim Refsnes

Kai Jim has been around computers since childhood, working with them since the age of 14.

He has been writing tutorials for w3schools since completing a bachelor's degree in information technology in 2005.

Jan Egil Refsnes

Jan Egil is the president and founder of w3schools.

He is a senior system developer with a master's degree in information technology and more than 30 years of computing experience.

"Jani" has supervised a large number of company-critical development projects for oil companies like Amoco, British Petroleum, ELF, Halliburton, and Brown & Root. He has also developed computer-based solutions for more than 20 governmental institutions like The National Library, Norwegian High Schools, The State Hospital, and many others.

Jani started w3schools in 1998.

Credits

Acquisitions Editor
Scott Meyers

Production
Abshier House

Copy Editor
Abshier House

Associate Director of Marketing
David Mayhew

Production Manager
Tim Tate

Proofreading and Indexing
Abshier House

Vice President and Executive Group Publisher
Richard Swadley

Vice President and Executive Publisher
Barry Pruett

Associate Publisher
Jim Minatel

Project Coordinator, Cover
Lynsey Stanford

Cover Designer
Michael Trent

TABLE OF CONTENTS

INTRODUCTION

Welcome to *Learn HTML and CSS with w3schools*. This book is for Web users learning to create their own Web pages using HTML, the standard tagging language for the World Wide Web.

w3schools (www.w3schools.com) is one of the top Web destinations to learn HMTL and many other key Web languages. w3schools' tutorials are recommended reading in more than 100 universities and high schools all over the world. This book is a great companion to the HTML and CSS tutorials on the w3schools site, which were written by Hege Refsnes, Ståle Refsnes, Kai Jim Refsnes, and Jan Egil Refsnes.

Like the w3schools online tutorials, this book features a brief presentation of each topic, trading lengthy explanations for abundant examples showcasing each key feature. This book, as well as other w3schools books published by Wiley, features straightforward and concise tutorials on each topic from which the beginning Web developer can easily learn. All of the book's content is derived from w3schools' accurate, user-tested content used by millions of learners every month.

HTML

With HTML, you can create your own Web site. HTML is the core technology in which all Web pages are written. This tutorial teaches you everything about HTML. HTML is easy to learn—you will enjoy it.

What You Should Already Know

Before you continue, you should have a basic understanding of how to use a browser to view pages on the Web.

If you want to study these subjects first, please read *The Internet For Dummies*, 12th Edition, also from Wiley Publishing.

What is HTML?

HTML is a language for describing Web pages.

- ▸▸ HTML stands for HyperText Markup Language.
- ▸▸ HTML is not a programming language, it is a markup language.
- ▸▸ A markup language is a collection of markup tags.
- ▸▸ HTML uses markup tags to describe Web pages.

What are Tags?

▸▸ HTML markup tags are usually called HTML tags or just tags.

▸▸ HTML tags are keywords surrounded by angle brackets like <html>.

▸▸ HTML tags normally come in pairs, like <b> and </b>.

▸▸ The first tag in a pair is the start tag; the second tag is the end tag.

▸▸ Start and end tags are also called opening tags and closing tags.

HTML Documents = Web Pages

▸▸ HTML documents describe Web pages.

▸▸ HTML documents contain HTML tags and plain text.

▸▸ HTML documents are also called Web pages.

The purpose of a Web browser (like Internet Explorer or Mozilla Firefox) is to read HTML documents and display them as Web pages. The browser does not display the HTML tags, but uses the tags to interpret the content of the page. In your browser, it looks like figure I.1.

```
<html>
<body>

<h1>My First Heading</h1>

<p>My first paragraph</p>

</body>
</html>
```

In the previous code example,

▸▸ The text between <html> and </html> describes the Web page.

▸▸ The text between <body> and </body> is the visible page content.

▸▸ The text between <h1> and </h1> is displayed as a heading.

▸▸ The text between <p> and </p> is displayed as a paragraph.

> **My First Heading**
>
> My first paragraph

Figure I.1

How to Use This Book

Throughout this book, you will see several icons:

Try it yourself >>

The Try It Yourself icon indicates an opportunity for you to practice what you've just learned. The code and examples under this icon come from examples on the w3schools site, which allow you to make changes to the code and see the results immediately. You do not have to type the code examples in this book; you can find them all on the w3schools site.

The w3schools icon indicates that more information is available on the w3schools site.

This icon indicates where you will find further information about a topic that is covered more thoroughly elsewhere within the book.

N O T E Notes call your attention to important information you need to know before proceeding.

T I P Tips provide you with suggested shortcuts and information to help you be more productive.

This book is divided into three sections:

▸▸ Section I: HTML Basic

▸▸ Section II: HTML/CSS Advanced

▸▸ Section III: Appendixes

If you're eager to improve your Web pages and to add some interactivity, jump right in with HTML basics. Plenty of examples and opportunities to try things await, and w3schools will be right there when you need them!

Section I
HTML Basic

CHAPTER 1

HTML GETTING STARTED

In This Chapter

❏ What You Need

❏ HTML Editors

❏ Create Your Own Test Web

❏ .HTM or .HTML Extension?

What You Need

It's simple to get started writing HTML.

▶▶ You don't need any tools to learn HTML with w3schools.

▶▶ You don't need an HTML editor.

▶▶ You don't need a Web server.

▶▶ You don't need a Web site.

HTML Editors

In this tutorial, we use a plain text editor (like Notepad) to edit HTML. We believe this is the best way to learn HTML.

Instead of writing plain text, however, professional Web developers often prefer using HTML editors like FrontPage or Dreamweaver because they offer code-writing shortcuts and helpful features.

Create Your Own Test Web

We suggest you experiment with everything you learn in this book by editing your Web files with a text editor (like Notepad) and opening them in Internet Explorer to view the results.

To create a test Web on your own computer, just copy the following three files from the w3schools Web site to your desktop.

http://www.w3schools.com/html/mainpage.htm
http://www.w3schools.com/html/page1.htm
http://www.w3schools.com/html/page2.htm

After you have copied the files, double-click on the file called mainpage.htm and see your first Web site in action.

If your test Web contains HTML markup tags you have not learned, don't panic.

You will learn all about markup tags in the next chapters.

.HTM or .HTML Extension?

When you save an HTML file, you can use either the .htm or the .html extension. We use .htm in our examples. It is a habit from the past, when the software only allowed three letters in file extensions.

In most cases, it is perfectly safe to use .html.

The w3schools Web site contains a wealth of helpful tools to help you learn HTML, including hundreds of cut-and-paste examples, an online text editor, an HTML Color Picker, quizzes to test your knowledge, and an abundance of Web-building reference tables. We recommend you refer to the Web site often as you work through this book. http://www.w3schools.com/html

CHAPTER 2

HTML FUNDAMENTALS

In This Chapter

- ❏ HTML Headings
- ❏ HTML Paragraphs
- ❏ HTML Links
- ❏ HTML Images

HTML Headings

HTML headings are defined with the <h1> to <h6> tags. The lower the number, the larger the heading size, as shown in Figure 2.1.

 Don't worry if the examples use tags you have not learned. You will learn more about tags in the next chapters.

Try it yourself >>

```
<html>
<body>

<h1>This is Heading 1</h1>
<h2>Heading 2 is Smaller</h2>
<h3>Heading 3 is Smaller Still</h3>

</body>
</html>
```

(continued)

9

(continued)

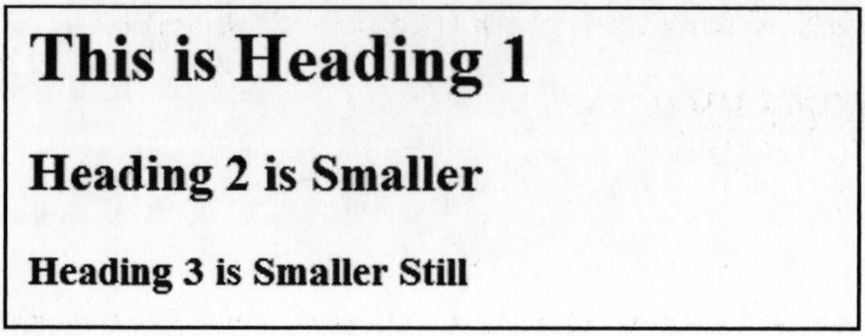

This is Heading 1

Heading 2 is Smaller

Heading 3 is Smaller Still

Figure 2.1

HTML Paragraphs

HTML paragraphs are defined with the <p> tag. Most browsers automatically put a line break and space after a </p> tag, as shown in Figure 2.2.

Try it yourself >>

```
<html>
<body>

<p>This is a paragraph.</p>
<p>This is a paragraph.</p>
<p>This is a paragraph.</p>

</body>
</html>
```

This is a paragraph.

This is a paragraph.

This is a paragraph.

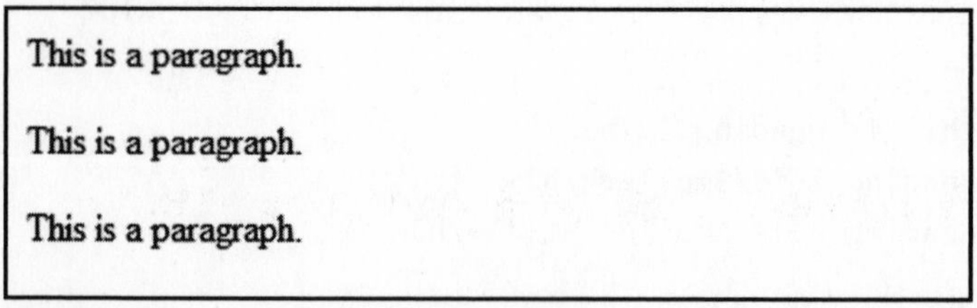

Figure 2.2

HTML Links

HTML links are defined with the <a> tag, as shown in Figure 2.3.

Try it yourself >>

```
<html>
<body>

<a href="http://www.w3schools.com">This is a link to the
  w3schools Web site.</a>

</body>
</html>
```

This is a link to the w3schools Web site.

Figure 2.3

 The URL address is an attribute of the link element. You will learn about attributes in Chapter 4, HTML Attributes.

HTML Images

HTML images are defined with the <img> tag. It tells the browser where to find the image file and what size to display it, among other things. The results of this code example are shown in Figure 2.4.

Try it yourself >>

```
<html>
<body>

<img src="w3schools.jpg" width="104" height="142" />

</body>
</html>
```

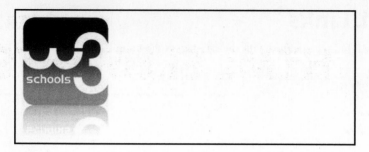

Figure 2.4

 The source name and size of the image are attributes of the image element. You will learn about attributes in Chapter 4, "HTML Attributes."

CHAPTER 3

HTML ELEMENTS

In This Chapter

- ❏ HTML Elements
- ❏ HTML Element Syntax
- ❏ Nested Elements
- ❏ Don't Forget the End Tag
- ❏ Empty HTML Elements
- ❏ Use Lowercase Tags

HTML Elements

HTML documents are defined by HTML elements. An HTML element is everything between the start tag and the end tag. The start tag is often called the opening tag. The end tag is often called the closing tag.

OPENING TAG	ELEMENT CONTENT	CLOSING TAG
<p>	This is a paragraph.	</p>
<a href="default.htm">	This is a link.	</a>

HTML Element Syntax

HTML elements follow a certain format regardless of how the element is used.

- ▶▶ An HTML element starts with a start tag/opening tag.
- ▶▶ An HTML element ends with an end tag/closing tag.
- ▶▶ The element content is everything between the start and the end tag.
- ▶▶ Some HTML elements have empty content.
- ▶▶ Empty elements are closed in the start tag.
- ▶▶ Most HTML elements can have attributes.

 You will learn more about attributes in Chapter 4, HTML Attributes.

13

Nested Elements

Most HTML elements can be nested (contain or be contained within other HTML elements). HTML documents consist of nested HTML elements.

The following example contains three HTML elements. Notice that the **<p>** element is nested in the **<body>** element, which in turn is nested in the **<html>** element. The results of these tags are shown in Figure 3.1.

```
<html>
<body>

<p>This is my first paragraph</p>

</body>
</html>
```

This is my first paragraph

Figure 3.1

The <p> element

The <p> element is among the most common of elements.

```
<p>This is my first paragraph</p>
```

▸ The <p> element defines a new paragraph in the HTML document.

▸ The element has a start tag <p> and an end tag </p>.

▸ The element content is: This is my first paragraph.

The <body> element

The <body> element defines the body of the HTML document.

```
<body>

<p>This is my first paragraph</p>

</body>
```

▸ The element has a start tag <body> and an end tag </body>.

▸ The element content is another HTML element (one or more paragraphs). There are usually dozens of elements within the body element.

The <html> element

The <html> element defines the entire HTML document.

```
<html>

<body>
<p>This is my first paragraph</p>
</body>

</html>
```

▸ The element has a start tag <html> and an end tag </html>.

▸ The element content is another HTML element (the body).

Don't Forget the End Tag

Most browsers will display HTML correctly even if you forget the end tag.

```
<p>This is a paragraph
<p>This is another paragraph
```

The previous example will work in most browsers, but don't rely on it. Forgetting the end tag can produce unexpected results or errors.

NOTE Future versions of HTML will not allow you to skip end tags.

Empty HTML Elements

HTML elements without content are called empty elements. Empty elements can be closed within the start tag.

 is an empty element without a closing tag. It defines a line break.

In XML and future versions of HTML, all elements must be closed.

Adding a slash to the end of start tag, like <br/>, is the proper way of closing empty elements, accepted by HTML, and XML.

Even if <br> works in all browsers, writing <br/> instead is more future proof.

Use Lowercase Tags

HTML tags are not case sensitive: <P> means the same as <p>. Plenty of Web sites use uppercase HTML tags in their pages.

w3schools uses lowercase tags because the World Wide Web Consortium (W3C) recommends lowercase in HTML 4.

CHAPTER 4

HTML ATTRIBUTES

In This Chapter

❑ Standard HTML Attributes

❑ Defining Attribute Values

❑ HTML Attributes Reference

Standard HTML Attributes

Attributes provide additional information about HTML elements.

▸▸ HTML elements can have attributes.

▸▸ Attributes provide additional information about the element.

▸▸ Attributes are always specified in the start tag.

▸▸ Attributes come in name/value pairs like: `name="value"`.

Defining Attribute Values

Attribute values should always be enclosed within quotation marks. While "double quotes" are the most common, single-style quotes (also called **primes**) are also allowed. In some rare situations, like when the attribute value itself includes quotation marks, it is necessary to use primes. For example:

```
name='John "Shotgun" Nelson'
```

As another example, HTML links are defined with the <a> tag. The Web address, surrounded by quotation marks, is the value of the attribute of the link element. The results appear in Figure 4.1.

```
<a href="http://www.w3schools.com">This is a link</a> to the
   w3schools Web site.
```

This is a link to the w3schools Web site.

Figure 4.1

TIP Attribute names and values are not case sensitive. However, the World Wide Web Consortium (W3C) recommends using lowercase attributes and values in its HTML 4 recommendation. Later versions require using lowercase.

HTML Attributes Reference

Table 4.1 lists some attributes that are standard for most HTML elements.

Table 4.1: Core Attributes

Attribute	Value	Description
class	class_rule or style_rule	The class of the element
id	id_name	A unique id for the element
style	style_definition	An inline style definition
title	tooltip_text	A text to display in a tool tip

NOTE A specific id may only appear once in a web page, while class refers to a class of elements that may appear many times in the same page.

The attributes listed in these references are standard and are supported by all HTML tags (with a few exceptions). A full list of legal attributes for each HTML element is listed in the w3schools Complete HTML Reference online at:

 http://www.w3schools.com/tags/default.asp

For more information about standard attributes, see the HTML Standard Attributes Reference online at:

 http://www.w3schools.com/tags/ref_standardattributes.asp

CHAPTER 5

HTML HEADINGS, RULES, & COMMENTS

In This Chapter

❑ HTML Headings

❑ HTML Rules (Lines)

❑ HTML Comments

❑ Viewing HTML Source Code

HTML Headings

Because users may skim your pages by their headings, it is important to use headings to show the document structure. Headings are defined, from largest to smallest, with the <h1> to <h6> tags.

H1 headings should be used as main headings, followed by H2 headings, then less important H3 headings, and so on. You can compare the appearance of the headings in Figure 5.1.

Try it yourself >>

```
<h1>This is a Heading 1</h1>
<h2>This is a Heading 2</h2>
<h3>This is a Heading 3</h3>
<h4>This is a Heading 4</h4>
<h5>This is a Heading 5</h5>
<h6>This is a Heading 6</h6>
```

This is a Heading 1

This is a Heading 2

This is a Heading 3

This is a Heading 4

This is a Heading 5

This is a Heading 6

Figure 5.1

Use HTML headings for headings only. Don't use headings to make text BIG or **bold**.

Search engines use your headings to index the structure and content of your Web pages.

> **NOTE** Browsers automatically add an empty line before and after headings.

HTML Rules (Lines)

The `<hr/>` tag is used to create a horizontal rule (line) across the browser page. Rules are often used to separate sections of a document, as shown in Figure 5.2, or to show a visual break.

Try it yourself >>

```
<html>
<body>

<p>The hr tag defines a horizontal rule:</p>
<hr />
<p>This is a paragraph</p>
<hr />
<p>This is a paragraph</p>
<hr />
<p>This is a paragraph</p>

</body>
</html>
```

The hr tag defines a horizontal rule:

This is a paragraph

This is a paragraph

This is a paragraph

Figure 5.2

HTML Comments

Comments can be inserted in the HTML code to make it more readable and understandable. Comments are ignored by the browser and are not displayed, as demonstrated in Figure 5.3.

Comments are written like this:

Try it yourself >>

```
<html>
<body>

<!--This comment will not be displayed-->
<p>This is a regular paragraph</p>

</body>
</html>
```

This is a regular paragraph

Figure 5.3

N O T E   Notice there is an exclamation point after the opening bracket, but not before the closing bracket.

21

Viewing HTML Source Code

Have you ever seen a Web page and wondered "Hey! How did they do that?" To find out, right-click in the page and select View Source (in Internet Explorer), View Page Source (in Firefox), or similar options for other browsers. This will open a window that shows you the HTML code of the page, as shown in Figure 5.4.

```
<!DOCTYPE html PUBLIC "-//W3C//DTD XHTML 1.0 Transitional//EN" "http://www.w
<html lang="en-US" xml:lang="en-US" xmlns="http://www.w3.org/1999/xhtml">
<head>
<title>Tryit Editor v1.4</title>
<link rel="stylesheet" type="text/css" href="/tryit.css" />
<script type="text/javascript">
function displayad()
{
document.getElementById("adframe").src="/tryitbanner.asp?secid=tryhtml&rnd="
}
</script>
</head>

<body>
<table width="100%" border="0" cellpadding="0" cellspacing="0">
<tr>
<td align="center">
<iframe id="adframe" style="background-color:#ffffff" height="98" width="890
src="/tryitbanner.asp?secid=tryhtml&rnd=0.3104364"></iframe>
</td>
</tr>
</table>
```

Figure 5.4

HTML Tag Reference

The tag reference for w3schools contains additional information about these tags and their attributes. A full list of legal attributes for each HTML element is listed in the w3schools Complete HTML Reference online at:

 http://www.w3schools.com/tags/default.asp

CHAPTER 6

HTML PARAGRAPHS

In This Chapter

- ❑ HTML Paragraphs
- ❑ HTML Line Breaks
- ❑ HTML Output Tips

HTML Paragraphs

HTML documents are divided into paragraphs. Paragraphs are defined with the
<p> tag.

```
<p>This is a paragraph.</p>
```

| NOTE | Most browsers automatically add an empty line before and after paragraphs. |

Don't Forget the End Tag

Most browsers will display HTML correctly even if you forget the end tag:

```
<p>This is a paragraph.
<p>This is another paragraph.</p>
```

This code will work in most browsers, but don't rely on it. Forgetting the end tag
can produce unexpected results or errors. Future versions of HTML will not allow
you to skip end tags.

HTML Line Breaks

Use the <br /> tag if you want a line break (a new line) without starting a new paragraph. The <br /> element is an empty HTML element. It has no end tag. The results of this code are shown in Figure 6.1.

```
<html>
<body>

<p>This is<br />a para-<br />graph with line breaks</p>

</body>
</html>
```

This is
a para-
graph with line breaks

Figure 6.1

N O T E   In XML and future versions of HTML, HTML elements with no end tag (closing tag) are not allowed. Even if <br> works in most browsers, writing <br /> instead is more future-proof and thus considered best practice.

HTML Output Tips

You can never be sure how HTML will be displayed. Large or small screens, different brands of browsers, and resized windows will create different results.

Be aware that with HTML, you cannot change the output by adding extra spaces or extra lines in your HTML code. The browser will remove extra spaces and extra lines when the page is displayed. Any number of lines count as one space, and any number of spaces count as as one space.

The following example shows how one might naturally think to format a passage of multiline text, but the results of that code, shown in Figure 6.2, remind you that the browser doesn't break the lines as you expect without a <br /> tag.

```
<html>
<body>

<p>
    My Bonnie lies over the ocean.
    My Bonnie lies over the sea.
    My Bonnie lies over the ocean.

    Oh, bring back my Bonnie to me.
</p>

<p>Note that your browser ignores your layout!</p>

</body>
</html>
```

My Bonnie lies over the ocean. My Bonnie lies over the sea. My Bonnie lies over the ocean. Oh, bring back my Bonnie to me.

Note that your browser ignores your layout!

Figure 6.2

The next example demonstrates some of the default behaviors of paragraph elements. As you can see in Figure 6.3, despite the fact that they were typed very differently, the first two paragraphs end up looking similar to the third paragraph, which had no extraneous spaces or line breaks.

```
<html>
<body>

<p>
This paragraph
contains a lot of lines
in the source code,
but the browser
```

(continued)

(continued)

```
ignores it.
</p>

<p>
This paragraph
contains      a lot of spaces
in the source     code,
but the     browser
ignores it.
</p>

<p>

The number of lines in a paragraph depends on the size of
   your browser window. If you resize the browser window, the
   number of lines in this paragraph will change.
</p>

</body>
</html>
```

This paragraph contains a lot of lines in the source code, but the browser ignores it.

This paragraph contains a lot of spaces in the source code, but the browser ignores it.

The number of lines in a paragraph depends on the size of your browser window. If you resize the browser window, the number of lines in this paragraph will change.

Figure 6.3

Complete Tag Reference

The w3schools tag reference contains additional information about these tags and their attributes. A full list of legal attributes for each HTML element is listed in the w3schools Complete HTML Reference online at:

 http://www.w3schools.com/tags/default.asp

CHAPTER 7

HTML TEXT FORMATTING

In This Chapter

HTML Formatting Tags

HTML uses tags like <b> and <i> to modify the appearance of text, like **bold** or *italic*. These HTML tags are called formatting tags. Refer to the end of this chapter for a complete reference.

Text Formatting

The following example demonstrates how you can format text in an HTML document. The results appear in Figure 7.1.

```
<html>
<body>

<p><b>This text is bold</b></p>
<p><strong>This text is strong</strong></p>
<p><big>This text is big</big></p>
<p><em>This text is emphasized</em></p>
<p><i>This text is italic</i></p>
<p><small>This text is small</small></p>
<p>This is<sub> subscript</sub> and <sup>superscript</sup></p>

</body>
</html>
```

This text is bold

This text is strong

This text is big

This text is emphasized

This text is italic

This text is small

This is $_{subscript}$ and ^{superscript}

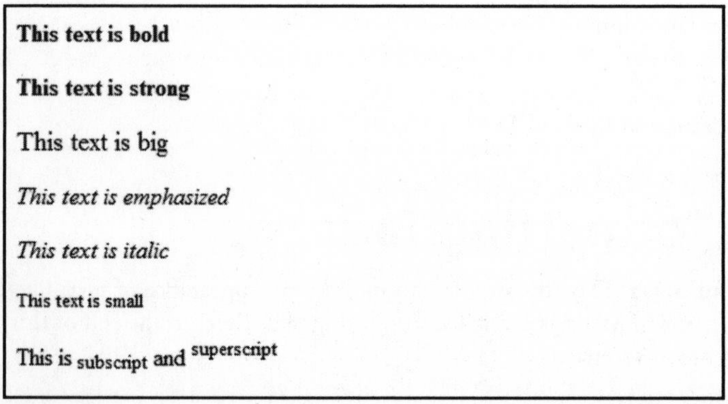

Figure 7.1

Preformatted Text

This example demonstrates how you can control the line breaks, spaces, and character widths with the <pre> tag.

 The results appear in Figure 7.2. You'll see more examples of computer output in the next section.

Try it yourself >>

```
<html>
<body>

<pre>
This is
preformatted text.
It preserves         both spaces
and line breaks and shows the text in a monospace font.
</pre>

<p>The pre tag is good for displaying computer code:</p>

<pre>
for i = 1 to 10
     print i
next i
</pre>

</body>
</html>
```

```
This is
preformatted text.
It preserves        both spaces
and line breaks and shows the text in a monospace font.

The pre tag is good for displaying computer code:

for i = 1 to 10
     print i
next i
```

Figure 7.2

"Computer Output" Tags

This example demonstrates how different "computer output" tags will be displayed. The results appear in Figure 7.3.

Try it yourself >>

```
<html>
<body>

<code>Computer code</code>
<br />
<kbd>Keyboard input</kbd>
<br />
<tt>Teletype text</tt>
<br />
<samp>Sample text</samp>
<br />
<var>Computer variable</var>
<br />

<p>
<b>Note:</b> These tags are often used to display computer/
    programming code on the page.
</p>

</body>
</html>
```

```
Computer code
Keyboard input
Teletype text
Sample text
Computer variable
```

Note: These tags are often used to display computer/programming code on the page.

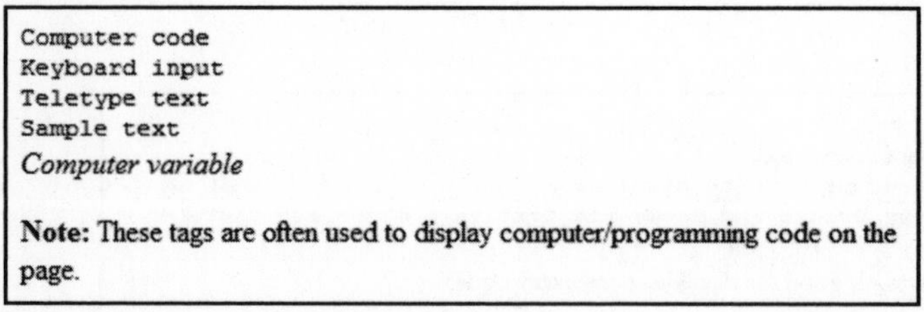

Figure 7.3

30

Address

This example demonstrates how to write an address in an HTML document. The results appear in Figure 7.4.

Try it yourself >>

```
<html>
<body>

<address>
Donald Duck<br>
BOX 555<br>
Disneyland<br>
USA
</address>

</body>
</html>
```

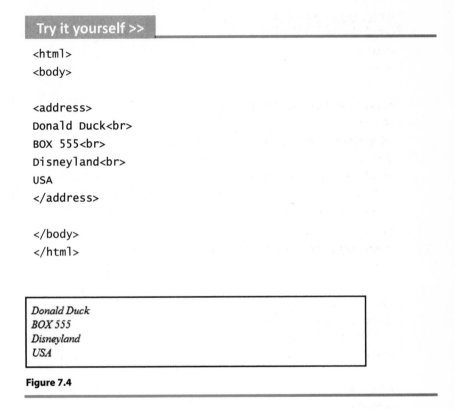

Donald Duck
BOX 555
Disneyland
USA

Figure 7.4

Abbreviations and Acronyms

This example demonstrates how to handle an abbreviation or an acronym. The results appear in Figure 7.5.

```
<html>
<body>

<abbr title="United Nations">UN</abbr>
<br />
<acronym title="World Wide Web">WWW</acronym>

<p>The title attribute is used to show the spelled-out
   version when holding the mouse pointer over the acronym
   or abbreviation.</p>

</body>
</html>
```

UN
WWW

The title attribute is used to show the spelled-out version when holding the
mouse pointer over the acronym or abbreviation.

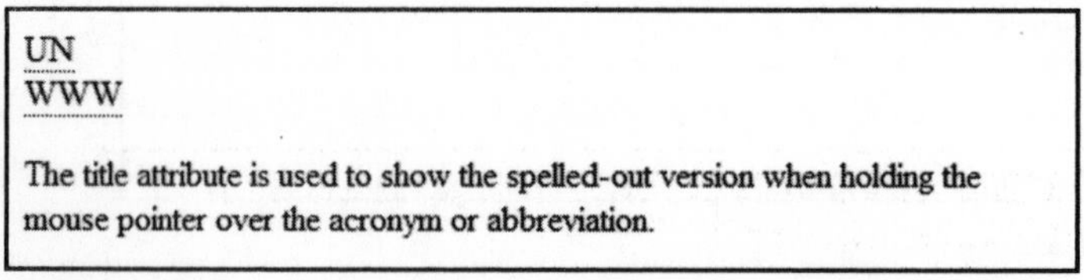

Figure 7.5

Text Direction

This example demonstrates how to change the text direction. The results appear in Figure 7.6.

Try it yourself >>

```
<html>
<body>

<p>
If your browser supports bidirectional override (bdo), the
  next line will be written from the right to the left
  (rtl):
</p>

<bdo dir="rtl">
Here is some backward text
</bdo>

</body>
</html>
```

> If your browser supports bidirectional override (bdo), the next line will be written from the right to the left (rtl):
>
> txet drawkcab emos si ereH

Figure 7.6

Quotations

This example demonstrates how to handle long and short quotations. The results appear in Figure 7.7.

```
<html>
<body>

A blockquote quotation:
<blockquote>
This is a long quotation. This is a long quotation. This is
   a long quotation. This is a long quotation. This is a long
   quotation.
</blockquote>

<p><b>The browser inserts line breaks and margins for a
   blockquote element.</b></p>

A short quotation:
<q>This is a short quotation</q>

<p><b>The q element does not render as anything special.</
   b></p>

</body>
</html>
```

A blockquote quotation:

> This is a long quotation. This is a long quotation. This is a long
> quotation. This is a long quotation. This is a long quotation.

The browser inserts line breaks and margins for a blockquote element.

A short quotation: "This is a short quotation"

The q element does not render as anything special.

Figure 7.7

Deleted and Inserted Text

This example demonstrates how to mark a text that is deleted (strikethrough) or inserted (underscore) to a document. The results appear in Figure 7.8.

```
<html>
<body>

<p>
a dozen is
<del>twenty</del>
<ins>twelve</ins>
pieces
</p>

<p>
Most browsers will <del>overstrike</del> deleted text and
  <ins>underscore</ins> inserted text.
</p>

<p>
Some older browsers will display deleted or inserted text as
  plain text.
</p>

</body>
</html>
```

a dozen is ~~twenty~~ twelve pieces

Most browsers will ~~overstrike~~ deleted text and underscore inserted text.

Some older browsers will display deleted or inserted text as plain text.

Figure 7.8

Text Formatting Tags

Examples of these tags' results appear in Figure 7.9.

> **N O T E**   Many of these tags are either deprecated or soon will be. Formatting with tags is very bad and should be done with CSS, and/or more descriptive content driven tags. Additionally, the <em>, <strong>, <dfn>, <code>, <samp>, <kbd>, <var>, and <cite> tags are all phrase tags. They are not deprecated, but it is possible to achieve richer effect with CSS.

TAG	DESCRIPTION
<b>	Defines bold text
<big>	Defines big text
<em>	Defines emphasized text
<i>	Defines italic text
<small>	Defines small text
<strong>	Defines strong text
<sub>	Defines subscripted text
<sup>	Defines superscripted text
<ins>	Defines inserted text
<del>	Defines deleted text
<s>	Deprecated. Use <del> instead
<strike>	Deprecated. Use <del> instead
<u>	Deprecated. Use styles instead

Defines bold text

Defines big text

Defines emphasized text

Defines italic text

Defines small text

Defines strong text

Defines subscripted text

Defines superscripted text

Defines inserted text

Defines deleted text

Figure 7.9

Computer Output Tags

Examples of these tags' results appear in Figure 7.10.

TAG	DESCRIPTION
<code>	Defines computer code text
<kbd>	Defines keyboard text
<samp>	Defines sample computer code
<tt>	Defines teletype text
<var>	Defines a variable
<pre>	Defines preformatted text
<listing>	Deprecated. Use <pre> instead
<plaintext>	Deprecated. Use <pre> instead
<xmp>	Deprecated. Use <pre> instead

```
Defines computer code text

Defines keyboard text

Defines sample computer code

Defines teletype text

Defines a variable

Defines preformatted text
```

Figure 7.10

Citations, Quotations, and Definition Tags

Examples of these tags' results appear in Figure 7.11.

TAG	DESCRIPTION
<abbr>	Defines an abbreviation
<acronym>	Defines an acronym
<address>	Defines an address element
<bdo>	Defines the text direction
<blockquote>	Defines a long quotation
<q>	Defines a short quotation
<cite>	Defines a citation
<dfn>	Defines a definition term

Defines an abbreviation

Defines an acronym

Defines an address element

Defines the text direction

> Defines a long quotation

"Defines a short quotation"

Defines a citation

Defines a definition term

Figure 7.11

CHAPTER 8

HTML STYLES

In This Chapter

- ❏ HTML Style Attribute
- ❏ Deprecated Tags and Attributes
- ❏ Common HTML Styles

The HTML Style Attribute

The style attribute is a new HTML attribute. It introduces the use of CSS in HTML. The purpose of the style attribute is to provide a common way to style all HTML elements.

Styles were introduced with HTML 4 as the new and preferred way to style HTML elements. With HTML styles, formatting and attributes can be added to HTML elements directly by using the style attribute, or indirectly in separate Cascading Style Sheets (CSS files).

 In this book, we use the style attribute to introduce you to HTML styles and CSS. You can learn more about styles and CSS in our tutorial, *Learn CSS with w3schools.*

The code in the following example and the results in Figure 8.1 introduce you to a new way of adding formatting to a document.

Try it yourself >>

```
<html>
<body style="background-color:Gray;">

<h1>Look! Styles and colors</h1>

<p style="font-family:verdana;color:red">
This text is in Verdana and red</p>

<p style="font-family:times;color:green">
```

```
This text is in Times and green</p>

<p style="font-size:30px">This text is 30 pixels high</p>

</body>
</html>
```

Look! Styles and colors

This text is in Verdana and red

This text is in Times and green

This text is 30 pixels high

Figure 8.1

 Because this book is not printed in color, it might be difficult to see the results dealing with in the figures. To see how the results look on the screen, enter this code into the Try It Yourself text editor at w3schools.com.

Deprecated Tags and Attributes

In HTML 4, some tags and attributes are defined as deprecated. Deprecated means that they will not be supported in future versions of HTML and The message is clear: Avoid the use of deprecated tags and attributes.

These tags and attributes should be avoided, and styles should be used instead:

TAGS	DESCRIPTION
<center>	Defines centered content
<font> and <basefont>	Defines HTML fonts
<s> and <strike>	Defines strikeout text
<u>	Defines underlined text
ATTRIBUTES	**DESCRIPTION**
align	Defines the alignment of text
bgcolor	Defines the background color
color	Defines the text color

Common HTML Styles

Background Color

```
<body style="background-color:gray">
```

The style attribute defines a style for the <body> element. The results of the style code appear in Figure 8.2.

Try it yourself >>

```
<html>
<body style="background-color:gray">
<h2>Look: Colored Background!</h2>

</body>
</html>
```

Look: Colored Background!

Figure 8.2

The new style attribute makes the "old" bgcolor attribute, shown in Figure 8.3, obsolete.

Try it yourself >>

```
<html>
<body bgcolor="gray">

<h2>Look: Colored Background!</h2>

<p>For future-proof HTML, use HTML styles instead:</p>
<p>style="background-color:gray"</p>

</body>
</html>
```

41

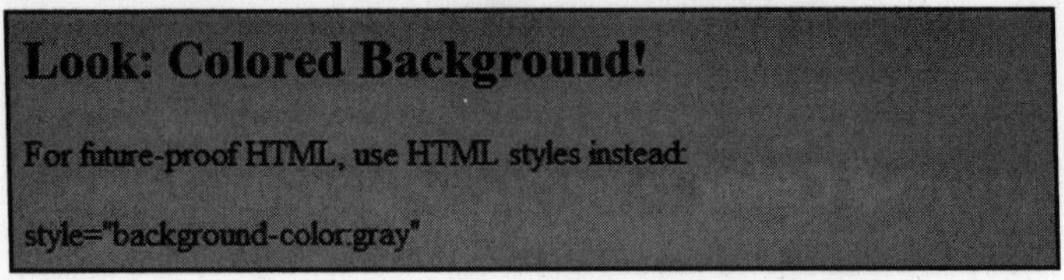
Look: Colored Background!
For future-proof HTML, use HTML styles instead:
style="background-color:gray"

Figure 8.3

Font Family, Color, and Size

The `style` attribute defines a style for the <p> element, as shown in Figure 8.4:

Try it yourself >>

```
<html>
<body>

<h1 style="font-family:verdana">A heading</h1>
<p style="font-family:courier new; color:red; font-
   size:20px;">A paragraph</p>

</body>
</html>
```

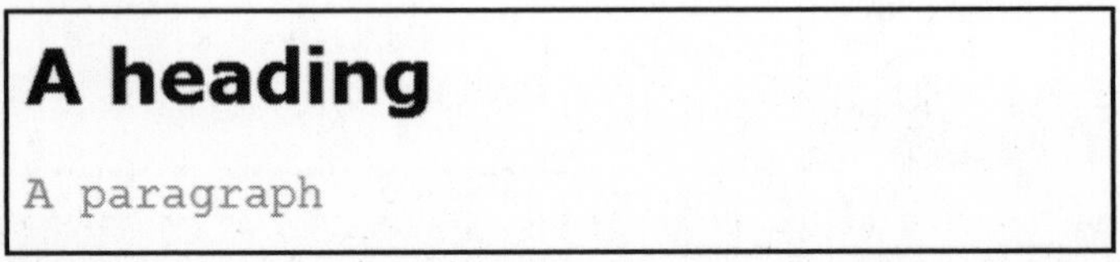
A heading
A paragraph

Figure 8.4

The new `style` attribute makes the old <font> tag, shown in Figure 8.5, obsolete.

Try it yourself >>

```
<html>
<body>

<p><font size="2" face="Verdana">
This is a paragraph.
</font></p>
```

```
<p><font size="5" face="Times" color="red">
This is another paragraph.
</font></p>

</body>
</html>
```

This is a paragraph.

This is another paragraph.

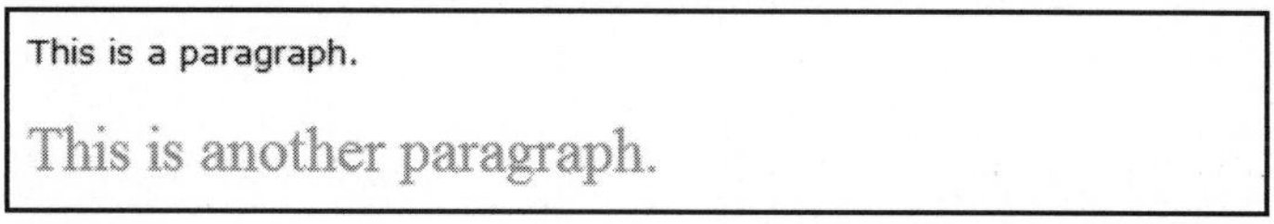

Figure 8.5

Text Alignment

```
<h1 style="text-align:center">
```

The `style` attribute defines a style for the `<h1>` element. The results appear in Figure 8.6.

Try it yourself >>

```
<html>
<body>

<h1 style="text-align:center">This is heading 1</h1>

<p>The heading above is aligned to the center of this page.
    The heading above is aligned to the center of this page.
    The heading above is aligned to the center of this page.
    </p>

</body>
</html>
```

This is heading 1

The heading above is aligned to the center of this page. The heading above is aligned to the center of this page. The heading above is aligned to the center of this page.

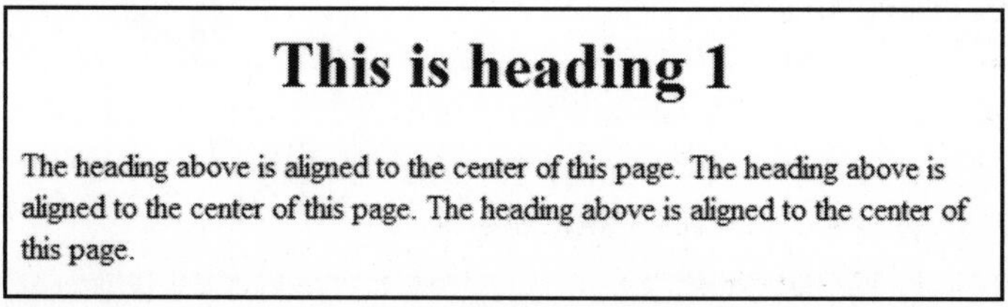

Figure 8.6

Although they display similarly in the browser, the new `style` attribute makes the old `align` attribute in Figure 8.7 obsolete.

```
<html>
<body>


<h1 align="center">This is heading 1</h1>

<p>The heading above is aligned to the center of this page.
   The heading above is aligned to the center of this page.
   The heading above is aligned to the center of this page.</
   p>

</body>
</html>
```

This is heading 1

The heading above is aligned to the center of this page. The heading above is aligned to the center of this page. The heading above is aligned to the center of this page.

Figure 8.7

Complete Tag Reference

The w3schools tag reference contains additional information about these tags and their attributes. A full list of legal attributes for each HTML element is listed in the w3schools Complete HTML Reference online at:

 http://www.w3schools.com/tags/default.asp

CHAPTER 9

HTML LINKS

In This Chapter

- ❏ HTML Links
- ❏ Open a Link in a New Browser Window
- ❏ Hyperlinks, Anchors, and Links
- ❏ HTML Link Syntax
- ❏ Links on the Same Page
- ❏ Creating a `mailto:` Link
- ❏ Creating an Image Link

HTML Links

A link is the "address" to a document (or a resource) located on the World Wide Web or elsewhere within your own Web server. Both types of links are shown in the following code example.

```
<html>
<body>

<p>
<a href="lastpage.htm">
This text</a> is a link to a page on this Web site.
</p>

<p>
<a href="http://www.microsoft.com/">
This text</a> is a link to a page on the World Wide Web.
</p>

</body>
</html>
```

You can see in Figure 9.1 that internal and external links are displayed similarly in the browser.

This text is a link to a page on this Web site.

This text is a link to a page on the World Wide Web.

Figure 9.1

Open a Link in a New Browser Window

The `target` attribute enables you to control how the browser responds when you click on the link. The following example demonstrates how to link to another page by opening a new window so that the visitor does not have to leave your Web site.

The results of the codes are shown in Figure 9.2.

Try it yourself >>

```
<html>
<body>

<a href="lastpage.htm" target="_blank">Last Page</a>

<p>
If you set the target attribute of a link to "_blank",
the link will open in a new window.
</p>

</body>
</html>
```

Last Page

If you set the target attribute of a link to "_blank", the link will open in a new window.

Figure 9.2

Hyperlinks, Anchors, and Links

In Web terms, a **hyperlink** is a reference (an address) to a resource on the Web. Hyperlinks can point to any resource on the Web: an HTML page, an image, a sound file, a movie, and so on.

An HTML **anchor** is a term used to define a hyperlink destination inside a document.

The anchor element **<a>** defines both hyperlinks and anchors.

> **N O T E**   We will use the term HTML link when the <a> element points to a resource, and the term HTML anchor when the <a> elements defines an address inside a document.

HTML Link Syntax

The start tag contains attributes about the link.

```
<a href="url">Link text</a>
```

The element content (Link text) defines the part to be displayed. The element content doesn't have to be text. You can link from an image or any other HTML element.

href Attribute

The href attribute defines the link "address". The following code will display in a browser as shown in Figure 9.3:

This <a> element defines a link to w3schools:

```
<a href="http://www.w3schools.com/">Visit w3schools!</a>
```

Visit w3schools!

Figure 9.3

The target Attribute

The target attribute defines where the linked document will be opened.

The following code example opens the document in a new browser window:

```
<html>
<body>

<a href=http://www.w3schools.com/ target="_blank">Visit
  w3schools!</a>

<p>
If you set the target attribute of a link to "_blank",
the link will open in a new window.
</p>

</body>
</html>
```

You can use the following options for the target attribute:

OPTION	DESCRIPTION
_blank	Opens the linked document in a new window
_self	Opens the linked document in the same frame as it was clicked (this is default)
_parent	Opens the linked document in the parent frameset
_top	Opens the linked document in the full body of the window
framename	Opens the linked document in a named frame

The name Attribute

When the name attribute is used, the <a> element defines a named anchor inside an HTML document. Named anchors are not displayed in any special way by the browser because they are invisible to the reader.

Named anchors are sometimes used to create a table of contents at the beginning of a large document. Each chapter within the document is given a named anchor, and links to each of these anchors are put at the top of the document.

If a browser cannot find a named anchor that has been specified, it goes to the top of the document. No error occurs.

Named anchor syntax:

```
<a name="label">Any content</a>
```

The link syntax to a named anchor:

```
<a href="#label">Any content</a>
```

The # in the href attribute defines a link to a named anchor. A named anchor inside an HTML document:

```
<a name="tips">Useful Tips Section</a>
```

A link to the "Useful Tips Section" from elsewhere in the same document:

```
<a href="#tips">Jump to the Useful Tips Section</a>
```

A link to the "Useful Tips Section" from another document:

```
<a href="http://www.w3schools.com/html_tutorial.
   htm#tips">Jump to the Useful Tips Section</a>
```

> **TIP** Always add a trailing slash to subfolder references. If you link like this: href="http://www.w3schools.com/html", you will generate two HTTP requests to the server because the server will add a slash to the address and create a new request like this: href="http://www.w3schools.com/html/".

Links on the Same Page

The following code example demonstrates how to use a link to jump to another part of a document. The results of the code are shown in Figure 9.4.

```
<html>
<body>

<p>
<a href="#C4">See also Chapter 4.</a>
</p>

<h2>Chapter 1</h2>
<p>This chapter explains ba bla bla</p>

<h2>Chapter 2</h2>
<p>This chapter explains ba bla bla</p>

<h2>Chapter 3</h2>
<p>This chapter explains ba bla bla</p>

<h2><a name="C4">Chapter 4</a></h2>
<p>This chapter explains ba bla bla</p>

<h2>Chapter 5</h2>
<p>This chapter explains ba bla bla</p>

<h2>Chapter 6</h2>
<p>This chapter explains ba bla bla</p>

<h2>Chapter 7</h2>
<p>This chapter explains ba bla bla</p>

<h2>Chapter 8</h2>
<p>This chapter explains ba bla bla</p>

<h2>Chapter 9</h2>
<p>This chapter explains ba bla bla</p>

<h2>Chapter 10</h2>
<p>This chapter explains ba bla bla</p>

<h2>Chapter 11</h2>
<p>This chapter explains ba bla bla</p>
```

```
<h2>Chapter 12</h2>
<p>This chapter explains ba bla bla</p>

<h2>Chapter 13</h2>
<p>This chapter explains ba bla bla</p>

<h2>Chapter 14</h2>
<p>This chapter explains ba bla bla</p>

<h2>Chapter 15</h2>
<p>This chapter explains ba bla bla</p>

<h2>Chapter 16</h2>
<p>This chapter explains ba bla bla</p>

<h2>Chapter 17</h2>
<p>This chapter explains ba bla bla</p>

</body>
</html>
```

See also Chapter 4.

Chapter 1

This chapter explains ba bla bla

Chapter 2

This chapter explains ba bla bla

Chapter 3

This chapter explains ba bla bla

Chapter 4

This chapter explains ba bla bla

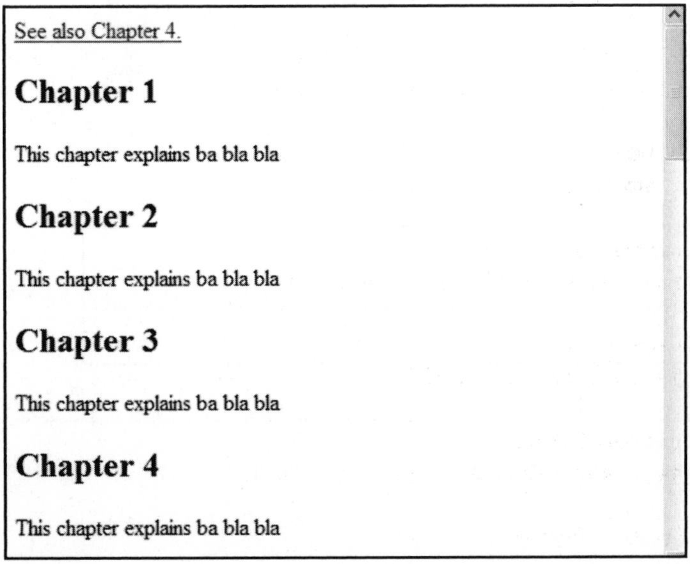

Figure 9.4

Creating a mailto: Link

The following example demonstrates how to link to an e-mail address and generate a new e-mail message in your default e-mail application (this works only if you have mail installed). The results of the code are shown in Figure 9.5.

Try it yourself >>

```
<html>
<body>

<p>
This is a mail link:
<a href="mailto:someone@microsoft.com?subject=Hello%20
   again">
Send Mail</a>
</p>

<p>
<b>Note:</b> Spaces between words should be replaced by %20
   to <b>ensure</b> that the browser will display your text
   properly.
</p>

</body>
</html>
```

This is a mail link: Send Mail

Note: Spaces between words should be replaced by %20 to **ensure** that the browser will display your text properly.

Figure 9.5

The following example demonstrates a more complicated `mailto:` link. This link not only generates a new e-mail, it adds a cc, bcc, a subject line, and the message body. The results of the code are shown in Figure 9.6.

```
<html>
<body>

<p>
This is another mailto link:
<a href="mailto:someone@microsoft.com?cc=someoneelse@
   microsoft.com&bcc=andsomeoneelse2@microsoft.
   com&subject=Summer%20Party&body=You%20are%20invited%20
   to%20a%20big%20summer%20party!">Send mail!</a>
</p>

<p>
<b>Note:</b> Spaces between words should be replaced by %20
   to <b>ensure</b> that the browser will display your text
   properly.
</p>

</body>
</html>
```

This is another mailto link: <u>Send mail!</u>

Note: Spaces between words should be replaced by %20 to **ensure** that the browser will display your text properly.

Figure 9.6

Creating an Image Link

The following example demonstrates how to use an image as a link. Click on the image to go to the linked page. The results of the code are shown in Figure 9.7.

```
<html>
<body>

<p>Create a link attached to an image:
<a href="default.htm">
<img src="smiley.gif" alt="HTML tutorial" width="32"
   height="32" />
</a></p>

<p>No border around the image, but still a link:
<a href="default.htm">
<img border="0" src="smiley.gif" alt="HTML tutorial"
   width="32" height="32" />
</a></p>

</body>
</html>
```

Create a link attached to an image:

No border around the image, but still a link:

Figure 9.7

You learn all about HTML images in Chapter 10, "HTML Images."

HTML IMAGES

In This Chapter

❏ img Tag and the src Attribute

❏ Insert Images from Different Locations

❏ Background Images

❏ Aligning Images

❏ Floating Images

❏ Adjusting Image Sizes

❏ alt Attribute

❏ Creating an Image Map

img Tag and the src Attribute

In HTML, images are defined with the <img> tag.

The img tag is empty, which means that it contains attributes only and it has no closing tag.

To display an image on a page, you need to use the src attribute. src stands for "source". The value of the src attribute is the URL of the image you want to display on your page.

The syntax of defining an image:

```
<img src="url" />
```

The URL points to the location or address where the image is stored. An image file named "boat.gif" located in the directory "images" on "www.w3schools.com" has the URL:

```
http://www.w3schools.com/images/boat.gif
```

> **NOTE** It is not necessary to have administrative access to the actual image file to which you are linking. You can link to any image as long as you know its URL.

The browser puts the image where the image tag occurs in the document. If you put an image tag between two paragraphs, the browser shows the first paragraph, then the image, and then the second paragraph.

The following example demonstrates how to insert images to your Web page. The results of this code are shown in Figure 10.1.

Try it yourself >>

```
<html>
<body>


<p>
An image:
<img src="constr4.gif" width="144" height="50" />
</p>


</body>
</html>
```

 An image:

Figure 10.1

N O T E   "Don't try this at home!" The images for this example reside on the w3schools server rather than your own, so unless you're using the Try It Yourself editor at www.w3shools.com, you won't get the same results. If you try this exact code in your browser the image will be missing.

The next section shows you how to point to images on other servers.

Insert Images from Different Locations

The example shown in Figure 10.2 demonstrates how to insert an image from another folder on your server or another location on the Web.

```
<html>
<body>

<p>An image from another folder:</p>
<img src="/images/chrome.gif" width="33" height="32" />

<p>An image from w3schools:</p>
<img src="http://www.w3schools.com/images/w3schools_green.
    jpg" width="104" height="142" />

</body>
</html>
```

An image from another folder:

An image from w3schools:

Figure 10.2

T I P Image files can take time to load in the browser, so use them sparingly.

Background Images

The next example demonstrates how to add a background image to an HTML page. The results appear in Figure 10.3.

```
<html>
<body background="background.jpg">

<h3>Look: A background image!</h3>

<p>Both gif and jpg files can be used as HTML backgrounds.</
   p>

<p>If the image is smaller than the page, the image will re-
   peat itself.</p>

</body>
</html>
```

Look: A background image!

Both gif and jpg files can be used as HTML backgrounds.

If the image is smaller than the page, the image will repeat itself.

Figure 10.3

Aligning Images

Figures 10.4 and 10.5 demonstrate different ways you can align images within the text.

```
<html>
<body>

<p>The text is aligned with the image
<img src="hackanm.gif" align="bottom" width="48" height="48"
    />
at the bottom.</p>

<p>The text is aligned with the image
<img src="hackanm.gif" align="middle" width="48" height="48"
    />
in the middle.</p>

<p>The text is aligned with the image
<img src="hackanm.gif" align="top" width="48" height="48" />
at the top.</p>

<p><b>Note:</b> The bottom alignment is the default!</p>

</html>
</body>
```

The text is aligned with the image at the bottom.

The text is aligned with the image in the middle.

The text is aligned with the image at the top.

Note: The bottom alignment is the default!

Figure 10.4

```
<html>
<body>

<p>This image appears
<img src="hackanm.gif" width="48" height="48" />
exactly where it is placed in the code.</p>

<p><img src="hackanm.gif" width="48" height="48" />
This image appears exactly where it is placed in the code.</
  p>

<p>This image appears exactly where it is placed in the
  code.
<img src="hackanm.gif" width="48" height="48" /></p>

</body>
</html>
```

This image appears exactly where it is placed in the code.

 This image appears exactly where it is placed in the code.

This image appears exactly where it is placed in the code.

Figure 10.5

Floating Images

In the next example, you learn how to let an image float to the left or right of a paragraph. The results appear in figure 10.6.

```
<html>
<body>

<p>
<img src="hackanm.gif" align="left" width="48" height="48"
    />
A paragraph with an image. The align attribute of the image
    is set to "left". The image will float to the left of this
    text.
</p>

<p>
<img src="hackanm.gif" align="right" width="48" height="48"
    />
A paragraph with an image. The align attribute of the im-
    age is set to "right". The image will float to the right of
    this text.
</p>

</body>
</html>
```

 A paragraph with an image. The align attribute of the image is set to "left". The image will float to the left of this text.

A paragraph with an image. The align attribute of the image is set to "right". The image will float to the right of this text.

Figure 10.6

Adjusting Image Sizes

The following example, shown in Figure 10.7, demonstrates how to display images in different sizes on the page.

The width and height attributes allow the page to render properly and more efficiently before the image is downloaded. Without them, the page will render once, then re-render when each image is loaded.

The image will be scaled to fit the stated height and width. Sometimes this can have a desired effect, other times it's disastrous.

Try it yourself >>

```
<html>
<body>

<p>
<img src="hackanm.gif" width="20" height="20" />
</p>

<p>
<img src="hackanm.gif" width="45" height="45" />
</p>

<p>
<img src="hackanm.gif" width="70" height="70" />
</p>

<p>You can make an image smaller or larger by changing the
   values of the height and width attributes.</p>

</body>
</html>
```

You can make an image smaller or larger by changing the values of the "height" and "width" attributes.

Figure 10.7

alt Attribute

The `alt` attribute is used to define an alternate text for an image. The `alt` attribute tells the reader what he or she is missing on a page if the browser can't load images. The browser will then display the alternate text instead of the image.

The value of the `alt` attribute is an author-defined text:

```
<img src="boat.gif" alt="Big Boat" />
```

It is a good practice to include alternate text for every image on a page to improve the display and usefulness of your document for people who have text-only browsers.

The following example shows what happens when the image file is not available. The results are in Figure 10.8.

Try it yourself >>

```
<html>
<body>

<p>
An image:
<img src="../constr4.gif" alt="Site_Under_Construction"
   width="200" height="50" />
</p>

</body>
</html>
```

🖼 "Site_Under_Construction"
An image:

Figure 10.8

Creating an Image Map

The following example demonstrates how to create an image map with clickable regions. Each of the regions is a hyperlink. The results of this example are shown in Figure 10.9.

 Creating a simple image link was covered in Chapter 9, "HTML Links".

```
<html>
<body>

<p>Click on the sun or on one of the planets to watch it
   closer:</p>

<img src="planets.gif" width="145" height="126" alt="Planets"
   usemap="#planetmap" />

<map name="planetmap">
   <area shape="rect" coords="0,0,82,126" alt="Sun" href="sun.
   htm" />
   <area shape="circle" coords="90,58,3" alt="Mercury"
   href="mercur.htm" />
   <area shape="circle" coords="124,58,8" alt="Venus"
   href="venus.htm" />
</map>

</body>
</html>
```

Click on the sun or on one of the planets to watch it closer:

Figure 10.9

Complete Tag Reference

w3schools' tag reference contains additional information about these tags and their attributes. A full list of legal attributes for each HTML element is listed in the w3schools Complete HTML Reference online at:

   http://www.w3schools.com/tags/default.asp

CHAPTER 11

HTML TABLES

In This Chapter

Creating HTML Tables

Tables are an excellent way to organize and display information on a page. Tables are defined using the `<table>` tag.

A table is divided into rows with the `<tr>` tag, and each row is divided into data cells using the `<td>` tag. The letters td stand for "table data," which is the content of a data cell. A data cell can contain text, images, lists, paragraphs, forms, horizontal rules, tables, and so on. A simple HTML table appears in Figure 11.1.

HTML Tables

Apples	44%
Bananas	23%
Oranges	13%
Other	10%

Figure 11.1

A basic table includes the following tags:

▸▸ Each table starts with a `table` tag.

▸▸ Each table row starts with a `tr` tag.

▸▸ Each table data (cell) starts with a `td` tag.

Following is an example of code for a table with one row and one column.

Try it yourself >>

```
<html>
<body>

<h4>One column:</h4>
<table border="1">
<tr>
  <td>100</td>
</tr>
</table>

</html>
</body>
```

The following code creates a table with one row and three columns.

```
<html>
<body>

<table border="1">
<tr>
  <td>100</td>
  <td>200</td>
  <td>300</td>
</tr>
</table>
</html>
</body>
```

The following code creates a table with two rows and three columns.

```
<html>
<body>

<table border="1">
<tr>
  <td>100</td>
  <td>200</td>
  <td>300</td>
</tr>
<tr>
  <td>400</td>
  <td>500</td>
  <td>600</td>
</tr>
</table>

</body>
</html>
```

The results of these three example tables appear in Figure 11.2.

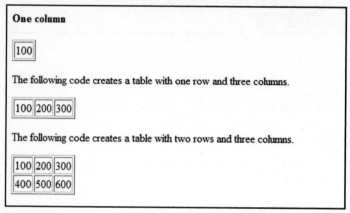

One column

100

The following code creates a table with one row and three columns.

100 200 300

The following code creates a table with two rows and three columns.

100 200 300
400 500 600

Figure 11.2

Table Borders

The border attribute controls the appearance of the table's borders or lines. The default border is 0, so if you do not specify a border attribute, the table is displayed without any borders. Sometimes this is useful, but most of the time, you want the borders to be visible. The following example demonstrates the use of different table borders. The results of this example are shown in Figure 11.3.

Try it yourself >>

```
<html>
<body>

<h4>With a normal border:</h4>
<table border="1">
<tr>
  <td>First</td>
  <td>Row</td>
</tr>
<tr>
  <td>Second</td>
  <td>Row</td>
</tr>
</table>

<h4>With a thick border:</h4>
<table border="8">
```

```
<tr>
  <td>First</td>
  <td>Row</td>
</tr>
<tr>
  <td>Second</td>
  <td>Row</td>
</tr>
</table>

<h4>With a very thick border:</h4>
<table border="15">
<tr>
  <td>First</td>
  <td>Row</td>
</tr>
<tr>
  <td>Second</td>
  <td>Row</td>
</tr>
</table>

</body>
</html>
```

With a normal border:

First	Row
Second	Row

With a thick border:

First	Row
Second	Row

With a very thick border:

First	Row
Second	Row

Figure 11.3

Table with No Border

If you don't provide a `border` attribute, the default is none. The following example shows two ways to create a table with no borders. Figure 11.4 displays the table as it appears in the browser. Figure 11.4 displays the table as it appears in the browser.

Try it yourself >>

```
<html>
<body>

<h4>This table has no borders:</h4>
<table>
<tr>
  <td>100</td>
  <td>200</td>
  <td>300</td>
</tr>
<tr>
  <td>400</td>
  <td>500</td>
  <td>600</td>
</tr>
</table>

<h4>This table also has no borders:</h4>
<table border="0">
<tr>
  <td>100</td>
  <td>200</td>
  <td>300</td>
</tr>
<tr>
  <td>400</td>
  <td>500</td>
  <td>600</td>
</tr>
</table>

</body>
</html>
```

This table has no borders:

100 200 300
400 500 600

This table also has no borders:

100 200 300
400 500 600

Figure 11.4

Headings in a Table

Table headings are defined with the <th> tag. Figure 11.5 shows the table as it appears in the browser.

Try it yourself >>

```
<html>
<body>

<table border="1">
<tr>
<th>Heading</th>
<th>Another Heading</th>
</tr>
<tr>
<td>row 1, cell 1</td>
<td>row 1, cell 2</td>
</tr>
<tr>
<td>row 2, cell 1</td>
<td>row 2, cell 2</td>
</tr>
</table>
<h4>Vertical headers:</h4>
<table border="1">
<tr>
  <th>First Name:</th>
```

(continued)

71

(continued)

```
  <td>Bill Gates</td>
</tr>
<tr>
  <th>Telephone:</th>
  <td>555 777 1854</td>
</tr>
<tr>
  <th>Telephone:</th>
  <td>555 777 1855</td>
</tr>
</table>

</body>
</html>
```

Heading	Another Heading
row 1, cell 1	row 1, cell 2
row 2, cell 1	row 2, cell 2

Vertical headers:

First Name:	Bill Gates
Telephone:	555 777 1854
Telephone:	555 777 1855

Figure 11.5

Empty Cells in a Table

Table cells with no content do not display very well in most browsers. Notice that the borders around the empty table cell are missing (except when using Mozilla Firefox). Figure 11.6 shows the table as it appears in the browser.

Try it yourself >>

```
<html>
<body>
```

```
<table border="1">
<tr>
<td>row 1, cell 1</td>
<td>row 1, cell 2</td>
</tr>
<tr>
<td>row 2, cell 1</td>
<td></td>
</tr>
</table>

</body>
</html>
```

row 1, cell 1	row 1, cell 2
row 2, cell 1	

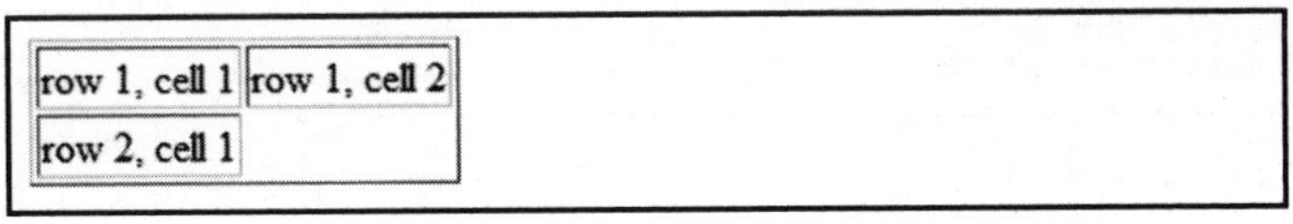

Figure 11.6

To avoid this, add a nonbreaking space ( ) to empty data cells to ensure the borders are visible, as shown in Figure 11.7.

Try it yourself >>

```
<table border="1">
<tr>
<td>row 1, cell 1</td>
<td>row 1, cell 2</td>
</tr>
<tr>
<td>row 2, cell 1</td>
<td> </td>
</tr>
</table>
```

73

row 1, cell 1	row 1, cell 2
row 2, cell 1	

Figure 11.7

TIP The <thead>, <tbody>, and <tfoot> elements are seldom used, because of bad browser support. Expect this to change in future versions of HTML.

Table with a Caption

The following example demonstrates how to create a table with a caption, as shown in Figure 11.8.

Try it yourself >>

```
<html>
<body>

<h4>This table has a caption, and a thick border:</h4>
<table border="6">
<caption>My Caption</caption>
<tr>
   <td>100</td>
   <td>200</td>
   <td>300</td>
</tr>
<tr>
   <td>400</td>
   <td>500</td>
   <td>600</td>
</tr>
</table>

</body>
</html>
```

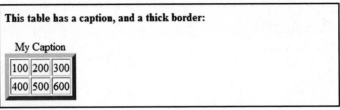

This table has a caption, and a thick border:

My Caption

| 100 | 200 | 300 |
| 400 | 500 | 600 |

Figure 11.8

Cells Spanning Multiple Columns

In this example, you learn how to define table cells that span more than one row or one column, as shown in Figure 11.9.

Try it yourself >>

```
<html>
<body>

<h4>Cell that spans two columns:</h4>
<table border="1">
<tr>
  <th>Name</th>
  <th colspan="2">Telephone</th>
</tr>
<tr>
  <td>Bill Gates</td>
  <td>555 77 854</td>
  <td>555 77 855</td>
</tr>
</table>

<h4>Cell that spans two rows:</h4>
<table border="1">
<tr>
  <th>First Name:</th>
  <td>Bill Gates</td>
</tr>
<tr>
  <th rowspan="2">Telephone:</th>
  <td>555 77 854</td>
```

(continued)

75

(continued)

```
 </tr>
 <tr>
   <td>555 77 855</td>
 </tr>
 </table>

 </body>
 </html>
```

Cell that spans two columns:

Name	Telephone	
Bill Gates	555 77 854	555 77 855

Cell that spans two rows:

First Name:	Bill Gates
Telephone:	555 77 854
	555 77 855

Figure 11.9

Tags Inside a Table

This example demonstrates how to display elements inside other elements. The results appear in Figure 11.10.

Try it yourself >>

```
<html>
<body>

<table border="1">
<tr>
  <td>
   <p>This is a paragraph</p>
   <p>This is another paragraph</p>
  </td>
  <td>This cell contains a table:
```

```
<table border="1">
<tr>
  <td>A</td>
  <td>B</td>
</tr>
<tr>
  <td>C</td>
  <td>D</td>
</tr>
</table>
</td>
</tr>
<tr>
<td>This cell contains a list
 <ul>
  <li>apples</li>
  <li>bananas</li>
  <li>pineapples</li>
 </ul>
</td>
<td>HELLO</td>
</tr>
</table>

</body>
</html>
```

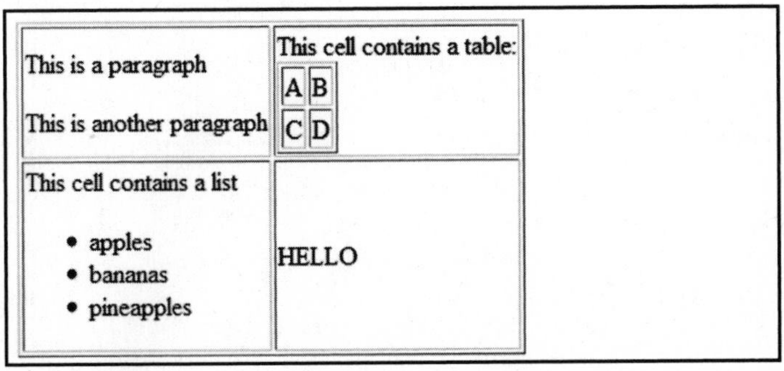

Figure 11.10

Cell Padding

This example demonstrates how to use cell padding to create more white space between the cell content and its borders. The results appear in Figure 11.11.

```
<html>
<body>

<h4>Without cellpadding:</h4>
<table border="1">
<tr>
  <td>First</td>
  <td>Row</td>
</tr>
<tr>
  <td>Second</td>
  <td>Row</td>
</tr>
</table>

<h4>With cellpadding:</h4>
<table border="1" cellpadding="10">
<tr>
  <td>First</td>
  <td>Row</td>
</tr>
<tr>
  <td>Second</td>
  <td>Row</td>
</tr>
</table>

</body>
</html>
```

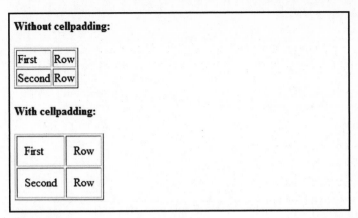

Figure 11.11

Cell Spacing

This example demonstrates how to use cell spacing to increase the distance between the cells, as shown in Figure 11.12

Try it yourself >>

```
<html>
<body>

<h4>Without cellspacing:</h4>
<table border="1">
<tr>
  <td>First</td>
  <td>Row</td>
</tr>
<tr>
  <td>Second</td>
  <td>Row</td>
</tr>
</table>

<h4>With cellspacing:</h4>
<table border="1" cellspacing="10">
<tr>
  <td>First</td>
```

(continued)

79

```
    <td>Row</td>
  </tr>
  <tr>
    <td>Second</td>
    <td>Row</td>
  </tr>
  </table>

</body>
</html>
```

Without cellspacing:

First	Row
Second	Row

With cellspacing:

First	Row
Second	Row

Figure 11.12

Table Background Colors and Images

This example demonstrates how to add a background to a table, as shown in Figure 11.13.

Try it yourself >>

```
<html>
<body>

<h4>A background color:</h4>
<table border="1" bgcolor="gray">
<tr>
  <td>First</td>
  <td>Row</td>
</tr>
<tr>
```

```
  <td>Second</td>
  <td>Row</td>
</tr>
</table>

<h4>A background image:</h4>
<table border="1" background="bgdesert.jpg">
<tr>
  <td>First</td>
  <td>Row</td>
</tr>
<tr>
  <td>Second</td>
  <td>Row</td>
</tr>
</table>

</body>
</html>
```

A background color:

A background image:

Figure 11.13

Cell Background Colors and Images

The following example demonstrates how to add a background to one or more table cells. The result is shown in Figure 11.14.

Try it yourself >>

```
<html>
<body>

<h4>Cell backgrounds:</h4>
<table border="1">
<tr>
  <td bgcolor="gray">First</td>
  <td>Row</td>
</tr>
<tr>
  <td background="bgdesert.jpg">
  Second</td>
  <td>Row</td>
</tr>
</table>

</body>
</html>
```

Cell backgrounds:

| First | Row |
| Second | Row |

Figure 11.14

Aligning Cell Content

This sample code demonstrates how to use the align attribute to align the content of cells to create a neatly organized table. The results of the code are shown in Figure 11.15.

Try it yourself >>

```
<html>
```

82

```
<body>

<table width="400" border="1">
 <tr>
  <th align="left">Money spent on....</th>
  <th align="right">January</th>
  <th align="right">February</th>
 </tr>
 <tr>
  <td align="left">Clothes</td>
  <td align="right">$241.10</td>
  <td align="right">$50.20</td>
 </tr>
 <tr>
  <td align="left">Make-Up</td>
  <td align="right">$30.00</td>
  <td align="right">$44.45</td>
 </tr>
 <tr>
  <td align="left">Food</td>
  <td align="right">$730.40</td>
  <td align="right">$650.00</td>
 </tr>
 <tr>
  <th align="left">Sum</th>
  <th align="right">$1001.50</th>
  <th align="right">$744.65</th>
 </tr>
</table>

</body>
</html>
```

Money spent on....	January	February
Clothes	$241.10	$50.20
Make-Up	$30.00	$44.45
Food	$730.40	$650.00
Sum	$1001.50	$744.65

Figure 11.15

frame Attribute

This example demonstrates how to use the frame attribute to control the borders around the table. The results of these examples appear in Figures 11.16 through 11.18. If you see no frames around the tables in your browser, either your browser is too old or it does not support the attribute.

Try it yourself >>

```
<html>
<body>

<h4>With frame="border":</h4>
<table frame="border">
<tr>
  <td>First</td>
  <td>Row</td>
</tr>
<tr>
  <td>Second</td>
  <td>Row</td>
</tr>
</table>

<h4>With frame="box":</h4>
<table frame="box">
<tr>
  <td>First</td>
  <td>Row</td>
</tr>
<tr>
  <td>Second</td>
  <td>Row</td>
</tr>
</table>

<h4>With frame="void":</h4>
<table frame="void">
<tr>
  <td>First</td>
  <td>Row</td>
</tr>
<tr>
  <td>Second</td>
  <td>Row</td>
</tr>
```

```
</table>

<html>
<body>
```

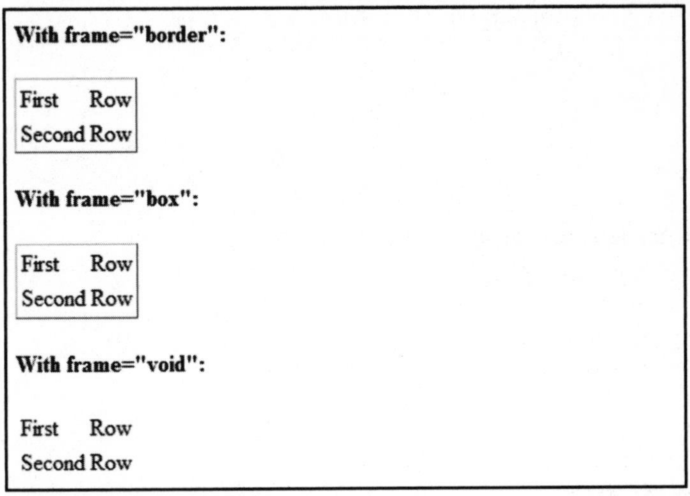

Figure 11.16

Try it yourself >>

```
<html>
<body>
<h4>With frame="above":</h4>
<table frame="above">
<tr>
  <td>First</td>
  <td>Row</td>
</tr>
<tr>
  <td>Second</td>
  <td>Row</td>
</tr>
</table>

<h4>With frame="below":</h4>
<table frame="below">
<tr>
```

(continued)

85

(continued)

```
    <td>First</td>
    <td>Row</td>
  </tr>
  <tr>
    <td>Second</td>
    <td>Row</td>
  </tr>
</table>

<h4>With frame="hsides":</h4>
<table frame="hsides">
<tr>
    <td>First</td>
    <td>Row</td>
</tr>
<tr>
    <td>Second</td>
    <td>Row</td>
</tr>
</table>
</body>
</html>
```

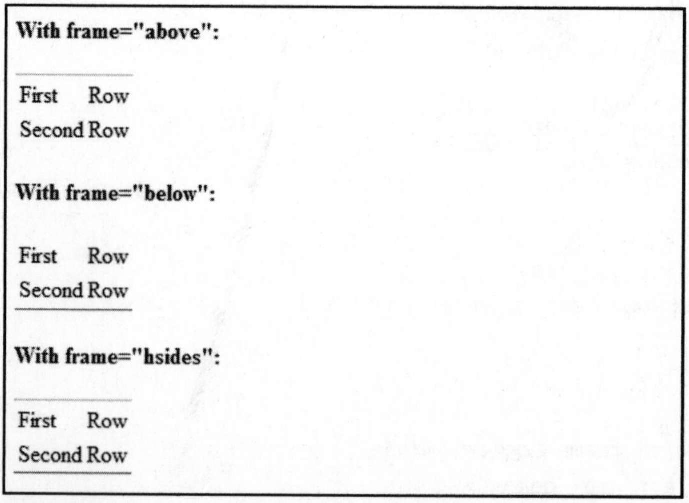

With frame="above":

First   Row
Second Row

With frame="below":

First   Row
Second Row

With frame="hsides":

First   Row
Second Row

Figure 11.17

86

Try it yourself >>

```
<html>
<body>
<h4>With frame="vsides":</h4>
<table frame="vsides">
<tr>
  <td>First</td>
  <td>Row</td>
</tr>
<tr>
  <td>Second</td>
  <td>Row</td>
</tr>
</table>

<h4>With frame="lhs":</h4>
<table frame="lhs">
<tr>
  <td>First</td>
  <td>Row</td>
</tr>
<tr>
  <td>Second</td>
  <td>Row</td>
</tr>
</table>

<h4>With frame="rhs":</h4>
<table frame="rhs">
<tr>
  <td>First</td>
  <td>Row</td>
</tr>
<tr>
  <td>Second</td>
  <td>Row</td>
</tr>
</table>
```

(continued)

(continued)
```
</body>
</html>
```

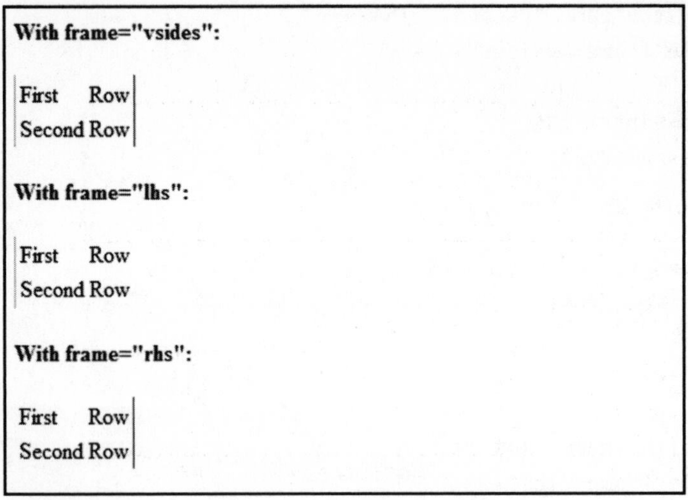

With frame="vsides":

First   Row
Second Row

With frame="lhs":

First   Row
Second Row

With frame="rhs":

First   Row
Second Row

Figure 11.18

Using frame and border to Control Table Borders

You can use the `frame` and `border` attributes to control the borders around the table. If you see no frames around the tables in these examples, your browser does not support the `frame` attribute.

Try it yourself >>

```
<html>
<body>

<table frame="hsides" border="3">
<tr>
  <td>First row</td>
</tr>
</table>
<br />
<table frame="vsides" border="3">
```

```
<tr>
  <td>First row</td>
</tr>
</table>

</body>
</html>
```

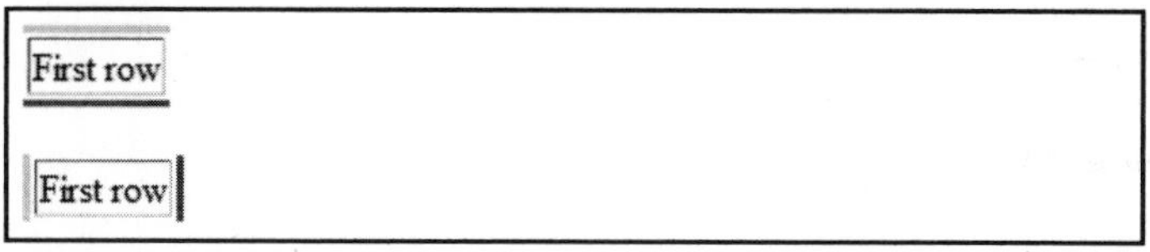

First row

First row

Figure 11.19

Table Tags

TAG	DESCRIPTION
<table>	Defines a table
<th>	Defines a table header
<tr>	Defines a table row
<td>	Defines a table cell
<caption>	Defines a table caption
<colgroup>	Defines groups of table columns
<col>	Defines the attribute values for one or more columns in a table
<thead>	Defines a table head
<tbody>	Defines a table body
<tfoot>	Defines a table footer

HTML LISTS

In This Chapter

❑ Unordered Lists

❑ Ordered Lists

❑ Definition Lists

❑ Nested Lists

Unordered Lists

HTML supports ordered, unordered, and definition lists. You can also nest one list within another.

An unordered list is a list of items. The list items are marked with bullets (typically small black circles), as shown in Figure 12.1.

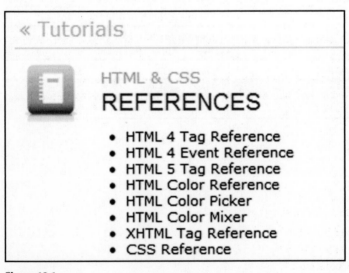

Figure 12.1

An unordered list starts with the <ul> tag. Each list item starts with the <li> tag. Figure 12.2 displays how it looks in a browser.

Try it yourself >>

```
<html>
<body>

<h4>An Unordered List:</h4>
<ul>
  <li>Coffee</li>
  <li>Tea</li>
  <li>Milk</li>
</ul>

</body>
</html>
```

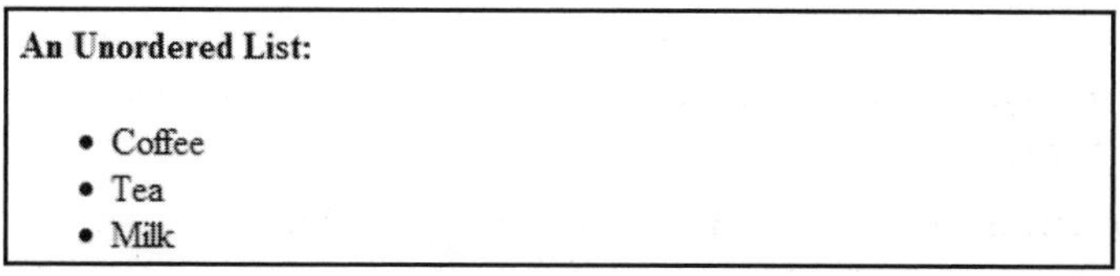

An Unordered List:

- Coffee
- Tea
- Milk

Figure 12.2

Inside a list item, you can put paragraphs, line breaks, images, links, other lists, and so on.

You can display different kinds of bullets in an unordered list by using the type attribute. Figure 12.3 shows lists marked with discs, circles, and squares.

Try it yourself >>

```
<html>
<body>

<h4>Disc bullets list:</h4>
<ul type="disc">
 <li>Apples</li>
 <li>Bananas</li>
 <li>Lemons</li>
</ul>
```

(continued)

(continued)

```
<h4>Circle bullets list:</h4>
<ul type="circle">
 <li>Apples</li>
 <li>Bananas</li>
 <li>Lemons</li>
</ul>

<h4>Square bullets list:</h4>
<ul type="square">
 <li>Apples</li>
 <li>Bananas</li>
 <li>Lemons</li>
</ul>

</body>
</html>
```

Disc bullets list:

- Apples
- Bananas
- Lemons

Circle bullets list:

○ Apples
○ Bananas
○ Lemons

Square bullets list:

▪ Apples
▪ Bananas
▪ Lemons

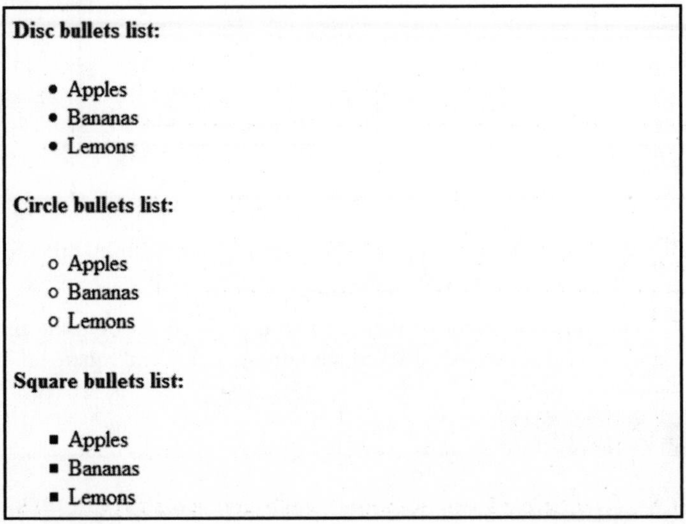

Figure 12.3

Ordered Lists

An ordered list is also a list of items; the list items are numbered sequentially rather than bulleted.

An ordered list starts with the `<ol>` tag. Each list item starts with the `<li>` tag. Figure 12.4 shows how the ordered list appears in the browser.

Try it yourself >>

```
<html>
<body>

<h4>An Ordered List:</h4>
<ol>
  <li>Coffee</li>
  <li>Tea</li>
  <li>Milk</li>
</ol>

</body>
</html>
```

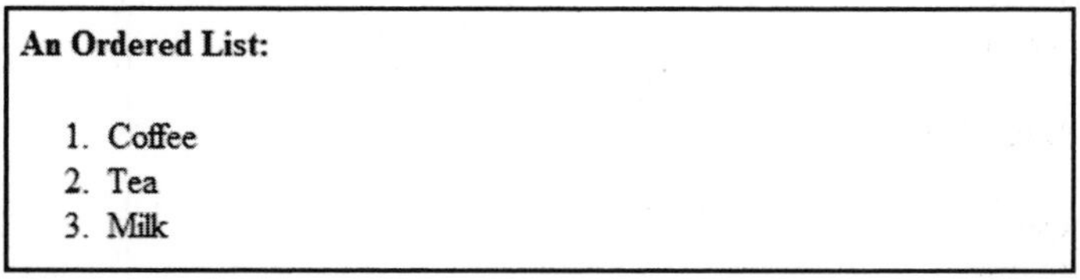

An Ordered List:

1. Coffee
2. Tea
3. Milk

Figure 12.4

Different Types of Ordering

You can display different kinds of ordered lists by using the `type` attribute. Figure 12.5 shows lists marked with uppercase and lowercase letters; Figure 12.6 shows lists with uppercase and lowercase Roman numerals.

Try it yourself >>

```
<html>
<body>
```

(continued)

93

(continued)

```
<h4>Letters list:</h4>
<ol type="A">
 <li>Apples</li>
 <li>Bananas</li>
 <li>Lemons</li>
</ol>

<h4>Lowercase letters list:</h4>
<ol type="a">
 <li>Apples</li>
 <li>Bananas</li>
 <li>Lemons</li>
</ol>

</body>
</html>
```

Letters list:

  A. Apples
  B. Bananas
  C. Lemons

Lowercase letters list:

  a. Apples
  b. Bananas
  c. Lemons

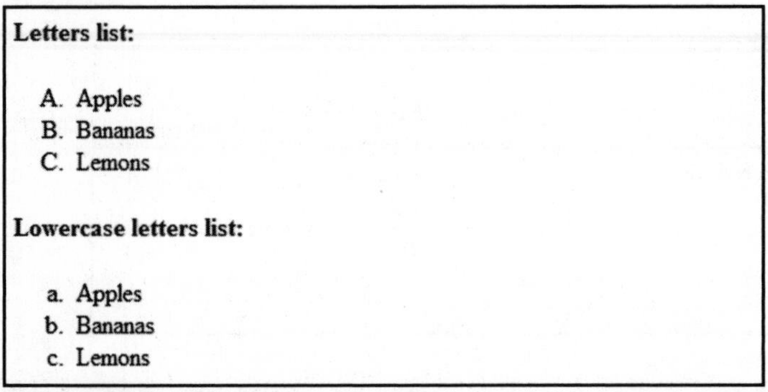

Figure 12.5

Try it yourself >>

```
<html>
<body>

<h4>Roman numbers list:</h4>
<ol type="I">
 <li>Apples</li>
 <li>Bananas</li>
 <li>Lemons</li>
```

```
</ol>

<h4>Lowercase Roman numbers list:</h4>
<ol type="i">
 <li>Apples</li>
 <li>Bananas</li>
 <li>Lemons</li>
</ol>

</body>
</html>
```

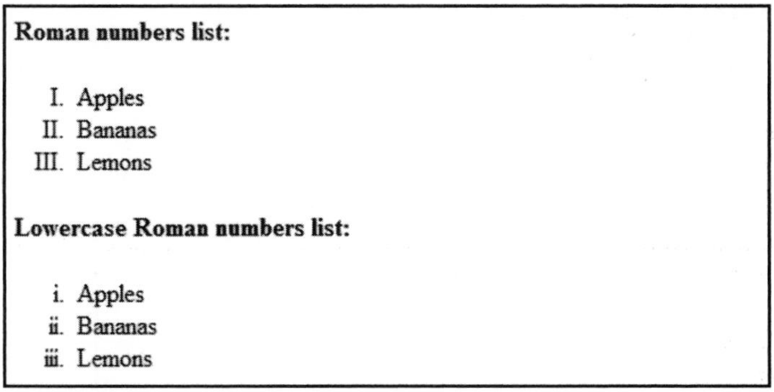

Roman numbers list:

  I. Apples
 II. Bananas
III. Lemons

Lowercase Roman numbers list:

  i. Apples
 ii. Bananas
iii. Lemons

Figure 12.6

Definition Lists

A definition list is not a list of single items. It is a list of items (terms), together with a description of each item (term).

A definition list starts with a <dl> tag (definition list).

Each term starts with a <dt> tag (definition term).

Each description starts with a <dd> tag (definition description).

Figure 12.7 shows how the definition list in the following example appears in a browser.

Try it yourself >>

```
<html>
<body>

<h4>A Definition List:</h4>
<dl>
  <dt>Coffee</dt>
  <dd>Black hot drink</dd>
  <dt>Milk</dt>
  <dd>White cold drink</dd>
</dl>

</body>
</html>
```

A Definition List:

Coffee
    Black hot drink
Milk
    White cold drink

Figure 12.7

Inside the <dd> tag you can put paragraphs, line breaks, images, links, other lists, and so on.

Nested Lists

A nested list is a list within another list. Usually the second list is indented another level and the item markers will appear differently than the original list, as shown in Figure 12.8.

Try it yourself >>

```
<html>
<body>

<h4>A nested List:</h4>
<ul>
  <li>Coffee</li>
```

```
<li>Tea
  <ul>
  <li>Black tea</li>
  <li>Green tea</li>
  </ul>
</li>
<li>Milk</li>
</ul>

</body>
</html>
```

A nested List:

- Coffee
- Tea
    - Black tea
    - Green tea
- Milk

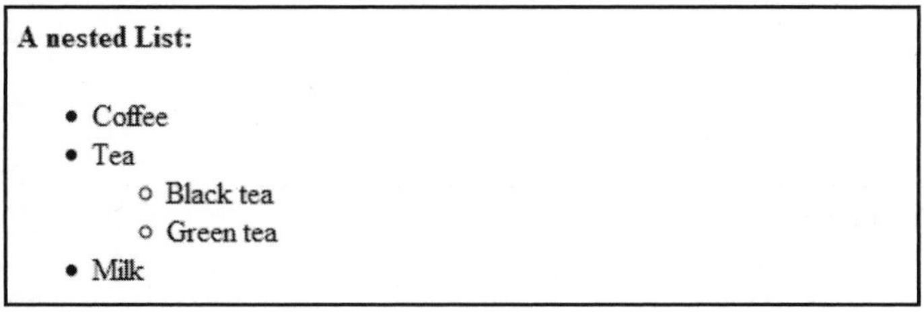

Figure 12.8

Nested lists can be several levels deep, as shown in Figure 12.9.

Try it yourself >>

```
<html>
<body>

<h4>A nested List:</h4>
<ul>
  <li>Coffee</li>
  <li>Tea
    <ul>
    <li>Black tea</li>
    <li>Green tea
      <ul>
      <li>China</li>
      <li>Africa</li>
      </ul>
    </li>
    </ul>
```

(continued)

(continued)
```
      </li>
    <li>Milk</li>
  </ul>

  </body>
  </html>
```

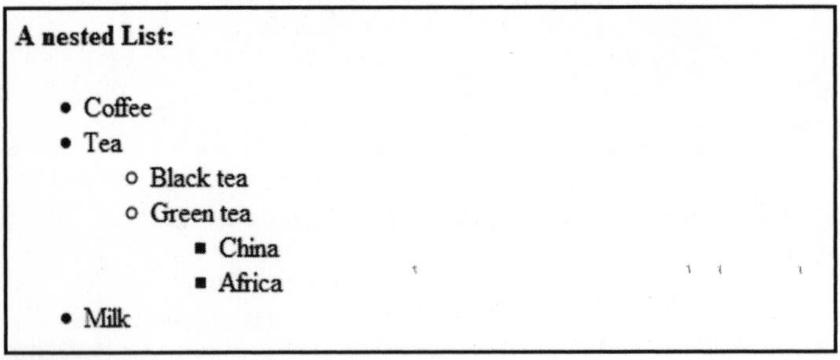

A nested List:

- Coffee
- Tea
  - Black tea
  - Green tea
    - China
    - Africa
- Milk

Figure 12.9

List Tags

TAG	DESCRIPTION
<ol>	Defines an ordered list
<ul>	Defines an unordered list
<li>	Defines a list item
<dl>	Defines a definition list
<dt>	Defines a term (an item) in a definition list
<dd>	Defines a description of a term in a definition list
<dir>	Deprecated. Use <ul> instead
<menu>	Deprecated. Use <ul> instead

HTML FORMS & INPUT

In This Chapter

❏ Forms

❏ `input` Tag and Attributes

❏ `action` Attribute

❏ Form Examples

Forms

HTML forms are used to collect different kinds of user input. A form is an area that can contain form elements.

Form elements are elements that allow the user to enter information in a form (like text fields, text area fields, drop-down menus, radio buttons, check boxes, and so on).

A simple form example appears in Figure 13.1.

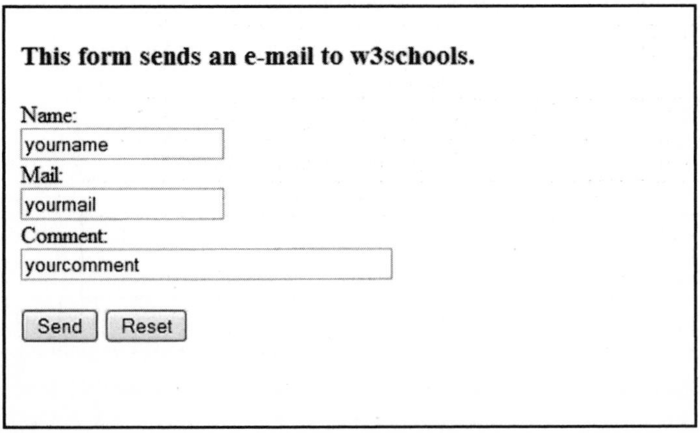

This form sends an e-mail to w3schools.

Name:
yourname
Mail:
yourmail
Comment:
yourcomment

Send   Reset

Figure 13.1

A form is defined with the `<form>` tag:

```
<form>
.
input elements
.
</form>
```

input Tag and Attributes

The most used form tag is the `<input>` tag. The type of input is specified with the type attribute. The following types are the most commonly used input types.

Text Fields

Text fields are used when you want the user to type letters, numbers, and so on in a form. The form appears as shown in Figure 13.2. Note that the form itself is not visible.

Try it yourself >>

```
<html>
<body>

<form action="">
First name:
<input type="text" name="firstname" />
<br />
Last name:
<input type="text" name="lastname" />
</form>

</body>
</html>
```

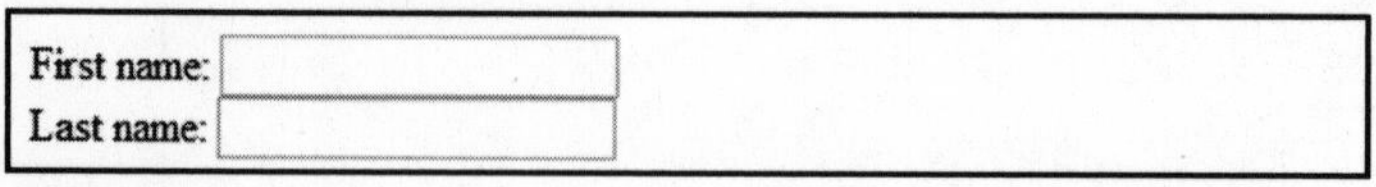

First name:
Last name:

Figure 13.2

TIP In most browsers, the width of the text field is 20 characters by default.

Check Boxes

This example demonstrates how to create check boxes on an HTML page like the ones shown in Figure 13.3. A user can select or deselect a check box.

Try it yourself >>

```
<html>
<body>

<form action="">
I have a bike:
<input type="checkbox" name="vehicle" value="Bike">
<br />
I have a car:
<input type="checkbox" name="vehicle" value="Car">
<br />
I have an airplane:
<input type="checkbox" name="vehicle" value="Airplane">
</form>

</body>
</html>
```

I have a bike: ☐
I have a car: ☐
I have an airplane: ☐

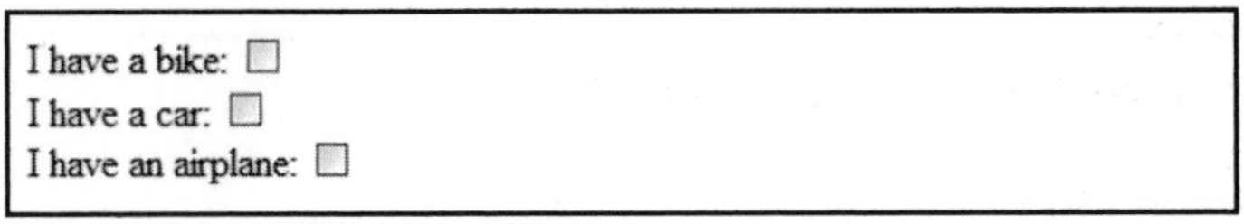

Figure 13.3

101

Radio Buttons

The example demonstrated in Figure 13.4 shows how to create radio buttons on an HTML form. When a user clicks a radio button, that button becomes selected, and all other buttons in the same group become deselected.

Try it yourself >>

```
<html>
<body>

<form action="">
Male:
<input type="radio" checked="checked"
name="Sex" value="male">
<br>
Female:
<input type="radio"
name="Sex" value="female">
</form>

</body>
</html>
```

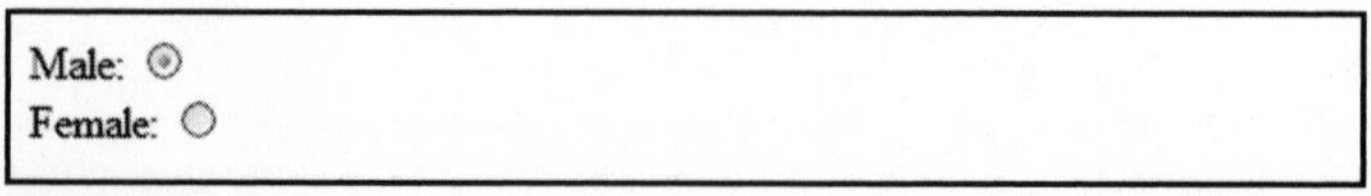

Male: ⊙
Female: ○

Figure 13.4

Drop-Down List

The next example shows how to create a simple drop-down list on an HTML page. A drop-down list is a selectable list.

Try it yourself >>

```
<html>
<body>

<form action="">
<select name="cars">
```

```
<option value="volvo">Volvo</option>
<option value="saab">Saab</option>
<option value="fiat">Fiat</option>
<option value="audi">Audi</option>
</select>
</form>

</body>
</html>
```

Figure 13.5

You can also display a simple drop-down list with a value preselected on the list, as shown in Figure 13.6.

```
<html>
<body>

<form action="">
<select name="cars">
<option value="volvo">Volvo</option>
<option value="saab">Saab</option>
<option value="fiat" selected="selected">Fiat</option>
<option value="audi">Audi</option>
</select>
</form>

</body>
</html>
```

Fiat ▾

Figure 13.6

Text Area

Using a textarea (a multiline text input control) like the one in Figure 13.7, you can write an unlimited number of characters. A textarea can be in a form or elsewhere on a page.

Try it yourself >>

```
<html>
<body>

<textarea rows="10" cols="30"> The cat was playing in the
   garden. </textarea>

</body>
</html>
```

```
 The cat was playing in the
garden.
```

Figure 13.7

Buttons

Buttons are common items on a form. This example demonstrates how to create a button. You can define your own text on the face of the button. The results of this code appear in Figure 13.8.

Try it yourself >>

```
<html>
<body>

<form action="">
<input type="button" value="Hello world!">
</form>
```

```
</body>
</html>
```

```
Hello world!
```

Figure 13.8

Fieldset

A fieldset is a grouping of data fields. This example demonstrates how to draw a border with a caption around your data, as shown in Figure 13.9.

```
<html>
<body>

<fieldset>
<legend>
Health information:
</legend>
<form action="">
Height <input type="text" size="3">
Weight <input type="text" size="3">
</form>
</fieldset>

<p>
If there is no border around the input form, your browser is
  too old.
</p>

</body>
</html>
```

┌─ Health information: ───┐
│ Height [   ] Weight [   ]   │
│   │
└───┘
If there is no border around the input form, your browser is too old.

Figure 13.9

action Attribute

When the user clicks the Submit button, the content of the form is sent to the server. The form's action attribute defines the name of the file to send the content to. The file defined in the action attribute usually does something with the received input.

```
<form name="input" action="html_form_submit.asp"
   method="get">
Username:
<input type="text" name="user" />
<input type="submit" value="Submit" />
</form>
```

Figure 13.10 shows how it looks in a browser. If you type some characters in the text field and click the Submit button, the browser sends your input to a page called "html_form_submit.asp". The page will show you the received input.

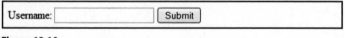

Figure 13.10

Form Examples

This example demonstrates how to add a form to a page. The form contains two input fields and a Submit button. The resulting form appears in Figure 13.11.

Try it yourself >>

```
<html>
<body>

<form name="input" action="html_form_action.asp"
   method="get">

Type your first name:
<input type="text" name="FirstName" value="Mickey" size="20">
<br>Type your last name:
<input type="text" name="LastName" value="Mouse" size="20">
<br>
<input type="submit" value="Submit">
```

```
</form>

<p>
If you click the "Submit" button, you will send your input
   to a new page called html_form_action.asp.
</p>

</body>
</html>
```

Type your first name:	Mickey
Type your last name:	Mouse

Submit

If you click the "Submit" button, you will send your input to a new page called html_form_action.asp.

Figure 13.11

Form with Check Boxes

The following form contains three check boxes and a Submit button. The results of the code appear in Figure 13.12.

Try it yourself >>

```
<html>
<body>

<form name="input" action="html_form_action.asp"
   method="get">
I have a bike:
<input type="checkbox" name="vehicle" value="Bike"
   checked="checked" />
<br />
I have a car:
<input type="checkbox" name="vehicle" value="Car" />
<br />
I have an airplane:
<input type="checkbox" name="vehicle" value="Airplane" />
<br /><br />
<input type="submit" value="Submit" />
</form>
```

(continued)

107

(continued)

```
<p>
If you click the "Submit" button, you send your input to a
   new page called html_form_action.asp.
</p>


</body>
</html>
```

```
I have a bike: ☑
I have a car: ☐
I have an airplane: ☐

 Submit

If you click the "Submit" button, you send your input to a new page called
html_form_action.asp.
```

Figure 13.12

Form with Radio Buttons

Figure 13.13 displays a form with two radio buttons and a Submit button.

Try it yourself >>

```
<html>
<body>

<form name="input" action="html_form_action.asp"
   method="get">
Male:
<input type="radio" name="Sex" value="Male"
   checked="checked">
<br>
Female:
<input type="radio" name="Sex" value="Female">
<br>
<input type ="submit" value ="Submit">
</form>


<p>
If you click the "Submit" button, you will send your input
```

```
to a new page called html_form_action.asp.
</p>

</body>
</html>
```

Male: ⊙
Female: ○
[Submit]

If you click the "Submit" button, you will send your input to a new page called
html_form_action.asp.

Figure 13.13

Send E-Mail from a Form

The next example demonstrates how to send e-mail from a form. The results of the
code appear in Figure 13.14.

Try it yourself >>

```
<html>
<body>
<form action="MAILTO:someone@w3schools.com" method="post"
  enctype="text/plain">

<h3>This form sends an e-mail to W3Schools.</h3>
Name:<br>
<input type="text" name="name"
value="yourname" size="20">
<br>
Mail:<br>
<input type="text" name="mail"
value="yourmail" size="20">
<br>
Comment:<br>
<input type="text" name="comment"
value="yourcomment" size="40">
<br><br>
<input type="submit" value="Send">
<input type="reset" value="Reset">
```

(continued)

109

(continued)

```
</form>
</body>
</html>
```

> **This form sends an e-mail to W3Schools.**
>
> Name:
> [yourname]
> Mail:
> [yourmail]
> Comment:
> [yourcomment]
>
> [Send] [Reset]

Figure 13.14

Form Tags

TAG	DESCRIPTION
<form>	Defines a form for user input
<input>	Defines an input field
<textarea>	Defines a textarea (a multiline text input control)
<label>	Defines a label to a control
<fieldset>	Defines a fieldset
<legend>	Defines a caption for a fieldset
<select>	Defines a selectable list (a drop-down box)
<optgroup>	Defines an option group
<option>	Defines an option in the drop-down box
<button>	Defines a pushbutton
<isindex>	Deprecated. Use `<input>` instead

HTML COLOR

In This Chapter

- ❏ Color Values
- ❏ 16 Million Different Colors
- ❏ Web Standard Color Names
- ❏ Color Names Supported by All Browsers
- ❏ Web Safe Colors?
- ❏ Shades of Gray

Color Values

HTML colors are defined using a hexadecimal (hex) notation for the combination of Red, Green, and Blue color values (RGB). The lowest value that can be given to one of the light sources is 0 (hex 00). The highest value is 255 (hex FF).

Hex values are written as three double-digit numbers, starting with a # sign, such as #9ACD32.

 Because this book is not printed in full color, it may be hard to see the some of the examples displayed in this chapter. You may want to consult the www.w3schools.com/html site to study working with color in HTML more closely.

The results of these codes are shown in Figure 14.1.

Color Values

COLOR	COLOR HEX	COLOR RGB
Black	#000000	rgb(0,0,0)
Red	#FF0000	rgb(255,0,0)
Green	#00FF00	rgb(0,255,0)
Blue	#0000FF	rgb(0,0,255)
Yellow	#FFFF00	rgb(255,255,0)
Cyan	#00FFFF	rgb(0,255,255)

(continued)

(continued)

Magenta	#FF00FF	rgb(255,0,255)
Gray	#C0C0C0	rgb(192,192,192)
White	#FFFFFF	rgb(255,255,255)

Try it yourself >>

```
<html>
<body>

<p style="background-color:#C0C0C0">
Color set by using hex value
</p>

<p style="background-color:rgb(192,192,192)">
Color set by using rgb value
</p>

<p style="background-color:gray">
Color set by using color name
</p>

</body>
</html>
```

Color set by using hex value

Color set by using rgb value

Color set by using color name

Figure 14.1

16 Million Different Colors

The combination of Red, Green and Blue values from 0 to 255 gives you a total of more than 16 million colors to play with (256 x 256 x 256). Most modern monitors are capable of displaying at least 16,384 colors.

If you look at the color table at http://www.w3schools.com/html/html_colors.asp, you will see the result of varying the red light from 0 to 255, while keeping the green and blue light at zero.

Web Standard Color Names

The World Wide Web Consortium (W3C) has listed 16 valid color names for HTML and CSS:

▸▸ Aqua

▸▸ Black

▸▸ Blue

▸▸ Fuchsia

▸▸ Gray

▸▸ Green

▸▸ Lime

▸▸ Maroon

▸▸ Navy

▸▸ Olive

▸▸ Purple

▸▸ Red

▸▸ Silver

▸▸ Teal

▸▸ White

▸▸ Yellow

If you want to use other colors, you should specify their HEX values.

Color Names Supported by All Browsers

The W3C HTML and CSS standards have listed only 16 valid color names. However, a collection of nearly 150 color names are supported by all major browsers.

 The complete list of color names supported by all major browsers is available on the w3schools Web site: http://www.w3schools.com/html/html_colornames.asp.

NOTE These additional names are not a part of the W3C Web standard. If you want valid HTML or CSS, use the HEX values instead.

Web Safe Colors?

Some years ago, when computers supported a maximum of 256 different colors, a list of 216 "Web Safe Colors" was suggested as a Web standard, reserving 40 fixed system colors. This cross-browser color palette was created to ensure that all computers would display the colors correctly when running a 256-color palette. This is not important now, because most computers can display millions of different colors.

 The complete list of Web Safe Colors is found at http://www.w3schools.com/html/html_colors.asp.

Shades of Gray

Gray colors are displayed using an equal amount of power to all of the light sources. To make it easier for you to select the right gray color, we have compiled the following table of gray shades.

 You will find the same table of gray shades at http://www.w3schools.com/html/html_colors.asp.\

GRAY SHADES	COLOR HEX	COLOR RGB
	#000000	rgb(0,0,0)
	#080808	rgb(8,8,8)
	#101010	rgb(16,16,16)
	#181818	rgb(24,24,24)
	#202020	rgb(32,32,32)
	#282828	rgb(40,40,40)
	#303030	rgb(48,48,48)
	#383838	rgb(56,56,56)
	#404040	rgb(64,64,64)
	#484848	rgb(72,72,72)
	#505050	rgb(80,80,80)
	#585858	rgb(88,88,88)
	#606060	rgb(96,96,96)
	#686868	rgb(104,104,104)
	#707070	rgb(112,112,112)
	#787878	rgb(120,120,120)
	#808080	rgb(128,128,128)

	#888888	rgb(136,136,136)
	#909090	rgb(144,144,144)
	#989898	rgb(152,152,152)
	#A0A0A0	rgb(160,160,160)
	#A8A8A8	rgb(168,168,168)
	#B0B0B0	rgb(176,176,176)
	#B8B8B8	rgb(184,184,184)
	#C0C0C0	rgb(192,192,192)
	#C8C8C8	rgb(200,200,200)
	#D0D0D0	rgb(208,208,208)
	#D8D8D8	rgb(216,216,216)
	#E0E0E0	rgb(224,224,224)
	#E8E8E8	rgb(232,232,232)
	#F0F0F0	rgb(240,240,240)
	#F8F8F8	rgb(248,248,248)
	#FFFFFF	rgb(255,255,255)

HTML 4.01 QUICK LIST

The following is an HTML Quick List from the first half of this book.

 You can view or print this quick list from the w3schools Web site at www. w3schools.com/html/html_quick.asp

HTML Basic Document

```
<html>
<head>
<title>Document name goes here</title>
</head>
<body>
Visible text goes here
</body>
</html>
```

Heading Elements

```
<h1>Largest Heading</h1>
<h2> . . . </h2>
<h3> . . . </h3>
<h4> . . . </h4>
<h5> . . . </h5>
<h6>Smallest Heading</h6>
```

Text Elements

```
<p>This is a paragraph</p>
<br /> (line break)
<hr /> (horizontal rule)
<pre>This text is preformatted</pre>
```

Logical Styles

```
<em>This text is emphasized</em>
<strong>This text is strong</strong>
<code>This is some computer code</code>
```

Physical Styles

```
<b>This text is bold</b>
<i>This text is italic</i>
```

Links, Anchors, and Image Elements

```
<a href="http://www.example.com/">This is a Link</a>
<a href="http://www.example.com/"><img src="URL"
   alt="Alternate Text"></a>
<a href="mailto:webmaster@example.com">Send e-mail</a>

A named anchor:
<a name="tips">Useful Tips Section</a>
<a href="#tips">Jump to the Useful Tips Section</a>
```

Unordered (Bulleted) List

```
<ul>
<li>First item</li>
<li>Next item</li>
</ul>
```

Ordered (Numbered) List

```
<ol>
<li>First item</li>
<li>Next item</li>
</ol>
```

Definition List

```
<dl>
<dt>First term</dt>
<dd>Definition</dd>
<dt>Next term</dt>
<dd>Definition</dd>
</dl>
```

Tables

```
<table border="1">
<tr>
<th>someheader</th>
<th>someheader</th>
</tr>
<tr>
<td>sometext</td>
<td>sometext</td>
</tr>
</table>
```

Frames

```
<frameset cols="25%,75%">
  <frame src="page1.htm">
  <frame src="page2.htm">
</frameset>
```

Forms

```
<form action="http://www.example.com/test.asp" method="post/
   get">
<input type="text" name="lastname" value="Nixon" size="30"
   maxlength="50">
<input type="password">
<input type="checkbox" checked="checked">
<input type="radio" checked="checked">
```

```
<input type="submit">
<input type="reset">
<input type="hidden">

<select>
<option>Apples
<option selected="selected">Apples</option>
<option selected>Bananas
<option selected="selected">Bananas</option>
<option>Cherries
<option>Cherries</option>
</select>
<textarea name="Comment" rows="60" cols="20"></textarea>

</form>
```

Entities

```
&lt; is the same as <
&gt; is the same as >
&#169; is the same as ©
```

Other Elements

```
<!-- This is a comment -->

<blockquote>
Text quoted from some source.
</blockquote>

<address>
Address 1<br>
Address 2<br>
City<br>
</address>
```
Source: http://www.w3schools.com/html/html_quick.asp.

Section II
HTML/CSS Advanced

CHAPTER 16

HTML LAYOUT

In this Chapter

❏ HTML Layout Using Tables

Everywhere on the Web, you find pages that are formatted like newspaper pages using HTML columns. One very common practice with HTML is to use HTML tables to format the layout of an HTML page.

HTML Layout Using Tables

A part of this page is formatted with two columns, like a newspaper page. As you can see on this page, there is a left column and a right column. This text is displayed in the left column.	An HTML `<table>` is used to divide a part of this Web page into two columns. The trick is to use a table without borders, and maybe a little extra cell padding. No matter how much text you add to this table, it will stay inside its column borders.

 For more information about creating and formatting tables, see "Chapter 11, "HTML Tables."

Dividing a part of an HTML page into table columns is very easy to do. Just set it up like the following example. The results are shown in Figure 16.1.

Try it yourself >>

```
<html>
<body>

<table border="0" width="100%" cellpadding="10">
<tr>
```

(continued)

(continued)

```
<td width="50%" valign="top">
This is some text. This is some text. This is some text.
   This is some text. This is some text.
</td>


<td width="50%" valign="top">
Another text. Another text. Another text. Another text. An-
   other text. Another text. Another text.
</td>


</tr>
</table>


</body>
</html>
```

This is some text. This is some text. This is some text. This is some text. This is some text.	Another text. Another text. Another text. Another text. Another text. Another text. Another text.

Figure 16.1

CHAPTER 17

HTML FRAMES

In This Chapter

- ❏ frameset Tag
- ❏ frame Tag
- ❏ Designing with Frames

With frames, you can display more than one HTML document in the same browser window. Each HTML document is called a **frame**, and each frame is independent of the others.

The disadvantages of using frames are:

▸▸ The web developer must keep track of more HTML documents.

▸▸ It is difficult to print the entire page.

▸▸ Users often dislike them.

▸▸ It presents linking challenges.

▸▸ People often use frames to wrap their own ads and branding around other people's content

frameset Tag

The <frameset> tag defines how to divide the window into frames. Each frameset defines a set of rows or columns. The values of the rows/columns indicate the amount of screen area each row/column will occupy.

Vertical Frameset

The following example demonstrates how to make a vertical frameset with three different documents. The results of the sample code appear in Figure 17.1

Try it yourself >>

```
<html>
<frameset cols="25%,50%,25%">
  <frame src="frame_a.htm">
  <frame src="frame_b.htm">
  <frame src="frame_c.htm">
</frameset>
</html>
```

Frame A	Frame B	Frame C

Figure 17.1

N O T E   Note that the code does not use the <body> tag when a <frame-set> tag is in use.

Horizontal Frameset

The following example demonstrates how to make a horizontal frameset with three different documents. The results of the sample code appear in Figure 17.2

Try it yourself >>

```
<html>

<frameset rows="25%,50%,25%">
  <frame src="frame_a.htm">
  <frame src="frame_b.htm">
  <frame src="frame_c.htm">
</frameset>

</html>
```

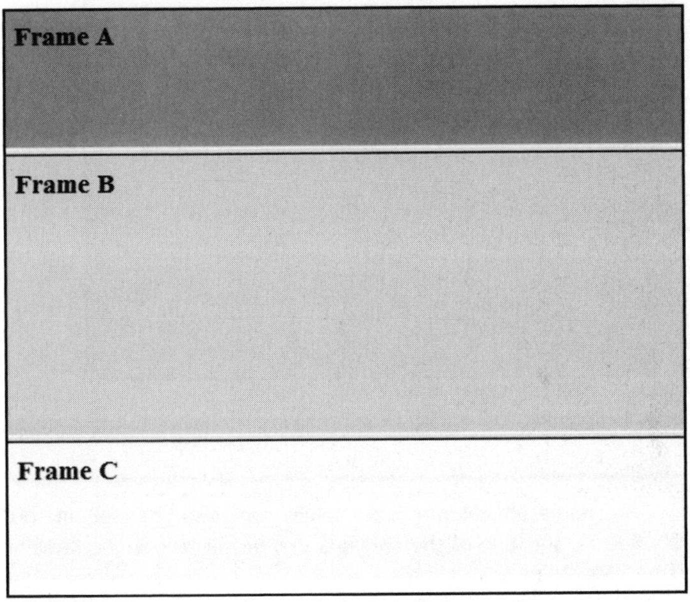

Frame A

Frame B

Frame C

Figure 17.2

frame Tag

The `<frame>` tag defines which HTML document will initially open in each frame.

In the following example, as shown in Figure 17.3, we have a frameset with two columns. The first column is set to 25% of the width of the browser window. The second column is set to 75% of the width of the browser window. The HTML document frame_a.htm is put into the first column, and the HTML document frame_b.htm is put into the second column.

127

Try it yourself >>

```
<frameset cols="25%,75%">
    <frame src="frame_a.htm">
    <frame src="frame_b.htm">
</frameset>
```

Frame A	Frame B

Figure 17.3

NOTE The frameset column size value can also be set in pixels (cols="200,500"), and one of the columns can be set to use the remaining space (cols="25%,*").

Designing with Frames

If a frame has visible borders, the user can resize it by dragging the border. To prevent a user from doing this, you can add noresize="noresize" to the <frame> tag.

noframes Tag

Although they are less common these days, it's a good idea to add the <noframes> tag for older or text-based browsers that do not support frames.

You cannot use the <body> tags together with the <frameset> tags. However, if you add a <noframes> tag containing some text for browsers that do not support frames, you will have to enclose the text in <body> tags. See how it is done in the following example. The results of this code appear in Figure 17.4.

Try it yourself >>

```
<html>

<frameset cols="25%,50%,25%">
  <frame src="frame_a.htm">
  <frame src="frame_b.htm">
  <frame src="frame_c.htm">

<noframes>
<body>Your browser does not handle frames!</body>
</noframes>

</frameset>

</html>
```

(This browser supports frames, so the noframes text remains invisible.)

Frame A	Frame B	Frame C

Figure 17.4

Mixed Frameset

The following example demonstrates how to make a frameset with three documents and how to mix them in rows and columns, as shown in Figure 17.5.

Try it yourself >>

```
<html>

<frameset rows="50%,50%">

<frame src="frame_a.htm">

<frameset cols="25%,75%">
<frame src="frame_b.htm">
<frame src="frame_c.htm">
</frameset>

</frameset>

</html>
```

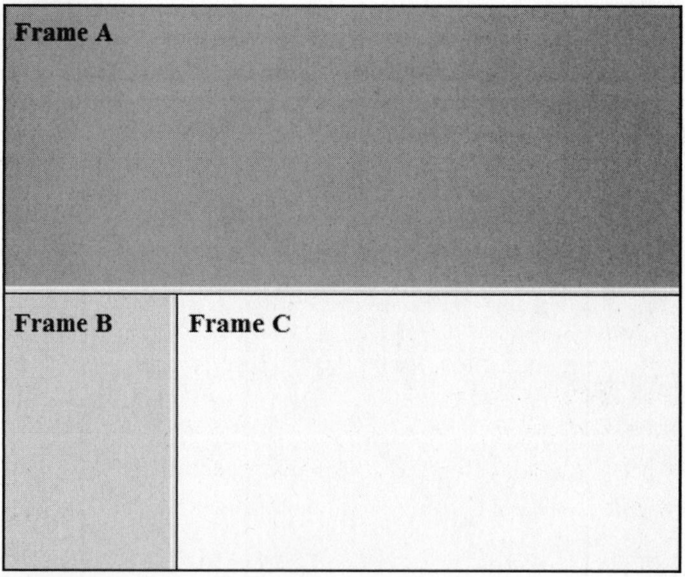

Frame A

Frame B   Frame C

Figure 17.5

noresize Attribute

This example demonstrates the `noresize` attribute. The frames are not resizable. Unlike other frames, if you move the mouse over the borders between the frames, you will notice that you cannot drag or move the frame borders.

Try it yourself >>

```
<html>


<frameset rows="50%,50%">
<frame noresize="noresize" src="frame_a.htm">


<frameset cols="25%,75%">
<frame noresize="noresize" src="frame_b.htm">
<frame noresize="noresize" src="frame_c.htm">


</frameset>


</html>
```

Navigation Frame

This example demonstrates how to make a navigation frame. A navigation frame contains a list of links with the second frame as the target. The second frame will show the linked document. A sample navigation frame appears in Figure 17.6.

Try it yourself >>

```
<html>


<frameset cols="120,*">
<frame src="tryhtml_contents.htm">
<frame src="frame_a.htm" name="showframe">
</frameset>


</html>
```

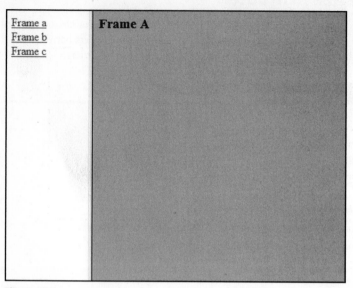

Figure 17.6

In the first column, the file called tryhtml_contents.htm contains links to three documents on the w3schools.com Web site. The source code for the links:

```
<a href ="frame_a.htm" target ="showframe">Frame a</a><br>
<a href ="frame_b.htm" target ="showframe">Frame b</a><br>
<a href ="frame_c.htm" target ="showframe">Frame c</a>
```

Inline Frame

Frames can also be used within a single HTML page. These are known as inline frames. The following example demonstrates how to create an inline frame like the one that appears in Figure 17.7.

Try it yourself >>

```
<html>
<body>

<iframe src="default.asp"></iframe>

<p>Some older browsers don't support iframes.</p>
<p>If they don't, the iframe will not be visible.</p>
```

```
</body>
</html>
```

Some older browsers don't support iframes.

If they don't, the iframe will not be visible.

Figure 17.7

Jump to

This example demonstrates two frames. One of the frames has a source to a specified section in a file. The specified section is made with <a name="C10"> in the link.htm file. The result is shown in Figure 17.8.

Try it yourself >>

```
<html>

<frameset cols="20%,80%">
 <frame src="frame_a.htm">
 <frame src="link.htm#C10">
</frameset>

</html>
```

133

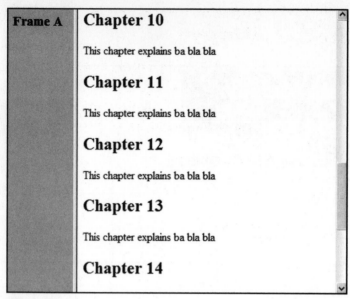

Figure 17.8

Jump to a Specified Section

This example demonstrates two frames. The navigation frame (content.htm) to the left contains a list of links with the second frame (link.htm) as a target on the right. The second frame shows the linked document. The result is shown in Figure 17.9.

```
<html>

<frameset cols="180,*">
<frame src="content.htm">
<frame src="link.htm" name="showframe">
</frameset>

</html>
```

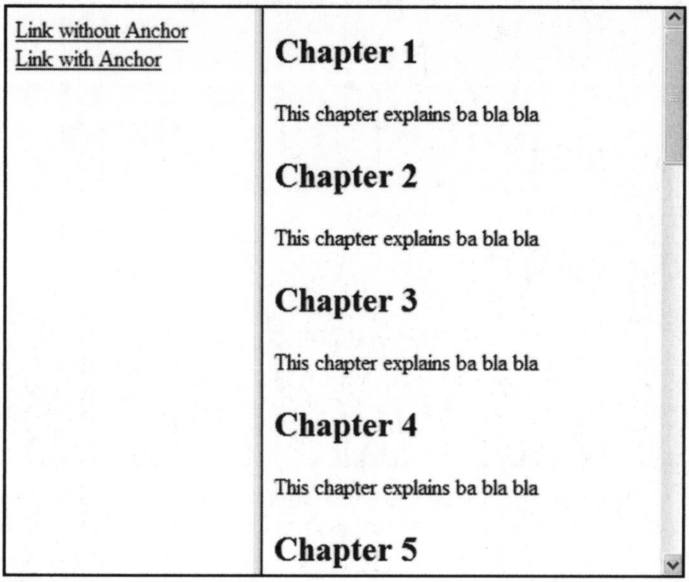

Figure 17.9

One of the links in the navigation frame is linked to a specified section in the target file. The HTML code in the file content.htm looks like this:

```
<a href ="link.htm" target ="showframe">Link without Anchor</
a><br><a href ="link.htm#C10" target ="showframe">Link
with Anchor</a>.
```

Frame Tags

TAG	DESCRIPTION
<frameset>	Defines a set of frames
<frame>	Defines a sub window (a frame)
<noframes>	Defines a noframe section for browsers that do not handle frames
<iframe>	Defines an inline sub window (frame)

CHAPTER 18

HTML FONTS

In This Chapter

❑ font Tag

❑ font Attributes

❑ Controlling Fonts with Styles

> **N O T E** The `<font>` tag in HTML is deprecated. It is supposed to be removed in a future version of HTML. Even if a lot of people are using it, you should try to avoid it and use styles instead. The tag is explained here to help you understand it if you see it used elsewhere on the Web.

font Tag

With HTML code like the following example, you can specify both the size and the type of the browser output. You can see what the results look like in Figure 18.1.

Try it yourself >>

```
<p>
<font size="2" face="Verdana">
This is a paragraph.
</font>
</p>
<p>
<font size="3" face="Times">
This is another paragraph.
</font>
</p>
```

This is a paragraph.

This is another paragraph.

Figure 18.1

Font Attributes

ATTRIBUTE	EXAMPLE	PURPOSE
size="number"	size="2"	Defines the font size
size="+number"	size="+1"	Increases the font size
size="-number"	size="-1"	Decreases the font size
face="face-name"	face="Times"	Defines the font name
color="color-value"	color="#eeff00"	Defines the font color
color="color-name"	color="red"	Defines the font color

Controlling Fonts with Styles

Although it's explained here, the <font> tag should not be used! The <font> tag is deprecated in the latest versions of HTML, which you learn more about in the next chapter.

The World Wide Web Consortium (W3C), an organization that creates and sets standards for the Web, has removed the <font> tag from its recommendations. In future versions of HTML, style sheets (CSS) will be used to define the layout and display properties of HTML elements.

Font

This example demonstrates how to set the font of a text, as shown in Figure 18.2.

Try it yourself >>

```
<html>
<body>
<h1 style="font-family:verdana">A heading</h1>
<p style="font-family:courier">A paragraph</p>
</body>
</html>
```

A heading

A paragraph

Figure 18.2

Font Size

This example demonstrates how to set the font size of a text, as shown in Figure 18.3.

Try it yourself >>

```
<html>
<body>
<h1 style="font-size:150%">A heading</h1>
<p style="font-size:80%">A paragraph</p>
</body>
</html>
```

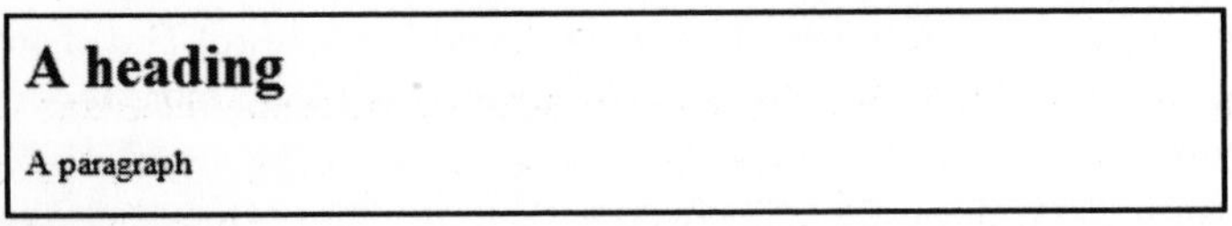

A heading

A paragraph

Figure 18.3

Font Color

This example demonstrates how to set the color of a text, as shown in Figure 18.4.

Try it yourself >>

```
<html>
<body>
<h1 style="color:blue">A blue heading</h1>
<p style="color:red">A red paragraph</p>
</body>
</html>
```

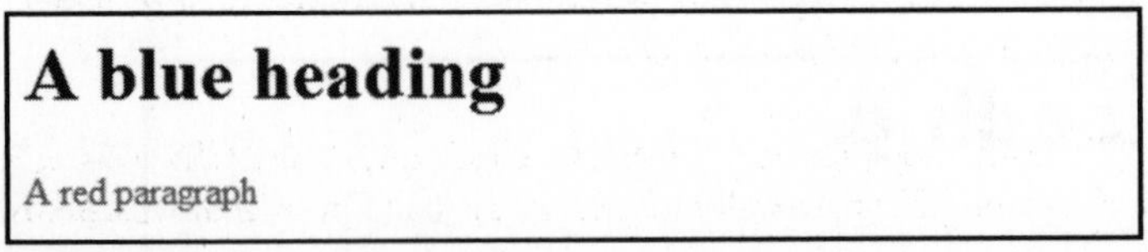

A blue heading

A red paragraph

Figure 18.4

The colors described in the code samples in this chapter are shown in grayscale in the figures. To see the full-color sample results, go to:

http://www.w3schools.com/html/html_fonts.asp

Font, Font Size, and Font Color

This example demonstrates how to set the font, font size, and font color of a text at the same time, as shown in Figure 18.5.

Try it yourself >>

```
<html>
<body>
<p style="font-family:verdana;font-size:80%;color:green">
This is a paragraph with some green text in it. This is a
   paragraph with some green text in it. This is a paragraph
   with some green text in it. This is a paragraph with some
   green text in it.
</p>
</body>
</html>
```

> This is a paragraph with some green text in it. This is a paragraph with some green text in it. This is a paragraph with some green text in it. This is a paragraph with some green text in it.

Figure 18.5

More About Style Sheets

The remaining chapters in this book focus on working with styles. In the following chapters, we will explain why some tags, like <font>, are to be removed from the HTML recommendations, and how to insert a style sheet in an HTML document.

To learn more about style sheets, check out *Learn CSS with w3schools*, also from Wiley Publishing, and try the CSS Tutorial at w3schools.com.

CHAPTER 19

WHY USE HTML 4.0?

In This Chapter

❏ HTML 3.2 Was Very Wrong!

❏ Enter HTML 4.0

HTML 3.2 Was Very Wrong!

The original HTML was never intended to contain tags for formatting a document. HTML tags were intended to define the content of the document like:

```
<p>This is a paragraph</p>
<h1>This is a heading</h1>
```

When tags like <font> and color attributes were added to the HTML 3.2 specification, it started a nightmare for Web developers. Development of large Web sites where fonts and color information had to be added to every single Web page, became a long, expensive, and unduly painful process.

Enter HTML 4.0

In HTML 4.0, all formatting can be removed from the HTML document and stored in a separate style sheet. Because HTML 4.0 separates the presentation from the document structure, you finally get what you always needed: total control of presentation layout without messing up the document content.

What Should You Do About It?

▸▸ Do not use presentation attributes inside your HTML tags if you can avoid it. Start using styles! Please read *Learn CSS with w3schools* to learn more about working with style sheets.

▸▸ Do not use deprecated tags. Visit the w3schools HTML 4.01 Reference to see which tags and attributes are deprecated:

http://www.w3schools.com/html/html_reference.asp

> **N O T E** The official HTML 4.01 recommends the use of lowercase tags.

Validate Your HTML Files as HTML 4.01

An HTML document is validated against a Document Type Definition (DTD). Before an HTML file can be properly validated, a correct DTD must be added as the first line of the file.

The HTML 4.01 Strict DTD includes elements and attributes that have not been deprecated or do not appear in framesets:

```
<!DOCTYPE HTML PUBLIC
"-//W3C//DTD HTML 4.01//EN"
"http://www.w3.org/TR/html4/strict.dtd">
```

The HTML 4.01 Transitional DTD includes everything in the strict DTD plus deprecated elements and attributes:

```
<!DOCTYPE HTML PUBLIC
"-//W3C//DTD HTML 4.01 Transitional//EN"
"http://www.w3.org/TR/html4/loose.dtd">
```

The HTML 4.01 Frameset DTD includes everything in the transitional DTD plus frames as well:

```
<!DOCTYPE HTML PUBLIC
"-//W3C//DTD HTML 4.01 Frameset//EN"
"http://www.w3.org/TR/html4/frameset.dtd">
```

Test Your HTML With the W3C Validator

If you want to check the markup validity of Web documents in HTML, input your page address (such as www.w3schools.com) in the box at the Markup Validation Service. The Validator is maintained by the W3C.

http://validator.w3.org/

CHAPTER 20

HTML CSS STYLES

In This Chapter

❏ Styles in HTML

❏ How to Use Styles

❏ Style Tags

Styles in HTML

With HTML 4.0, all formatting can be moved out of the HTML document and into a separate style sheet. This makes creating, updating, and maintaining the Web site much easier.

The following example demonstrates how to format an HTML document with style information added to the **<head>** section. The results of the sample code appear in Figure 20.1.

Try it yourself >>

```
<html>
<head>

<style type="text/css">
h1 {color: red}
h3 {color: blue}
</style>

</head>

<body>
<h1>This is header 1</h1>
<h3>This is header 3</h3>
</body>

</html>
```

This is header 1

This is header 3

Figure 20.1

Nonunderlined Link

Links are underlined by default in the browser page. The following example demonstrates how to display a link that is not underlined by default, using a `style` attribute. The results of the sample code appear in Figure 20.2.

Try it yourself >>

```
<html>
<body>

<a href="lastpage.htm"
style="text-decoration:none">
THIS IS A LINK!
</a>

</body>
</html>
```

THIS IS A LINK!

Figure 20.2

Link to an External Style Sheet

This example demonstrates how to use the <link> tag to link to an external style sheet. The results of the sample code appear in Figure 20.3.

Try it yourself >>

```
<html>
<head>
<link rel="stylesheet" type="text/css" href="styles.css" >
</head>

<body>
<h1>I am formatted with a linked style sheet</h1>
<p>Me too!</p>
</body>

</html>
```

I am formatted with a linked style sheet

Me too!

Figure 20.3

 The linked style sheets in the sample codes in this chapter are located on the w3schools.com server, so the sample code works best if you use the Try It Yourself editor. Go to http://www.w3schools.com/html and click Try it yourself.

How to Use Styles

When a browser reads a style sheet, it formats the document according to the instructions in the sheet. There are three types of style sheets: external, internal, and inline.

External Style Sheet

An external style sheet is ideal when the style is applied to many pages. With an external style sheet, you can change the look of an entire Web site by changing one file. Each page must link to the style sheet using the <link> tag. The <link> tag goes inside the <head> section.

```
<head>
<link rel="stylesheet" type="text/css" href="mystyle.css">
</head>
```

Internal Style Sheet

An internal style sheet should be used when a single document has a unique style. You define internal styles in the <head> section with the <style> tag. The results of the sample code appear in Figure 20.4.

Try it yourself >>

```
<head>
<style type="text/css">
body {background-color: gray}
p {margin-left: 20px}
</style>
</head>
<p>The left margin is indented 20 pixels.</p>
```

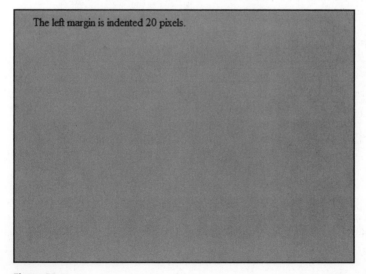

Figure 20.4

145

Inline Styles

An inline style should be used when a unique style is to be applied to a single occurrence of an element. To use inline styles, you use the `style` attribute in the relevant tag. The `style` attribute can contain any CSS property.

The example shown in Figure 20.5 demonstrates how to change the background color and the left margin of a paragraph.

Try it yourself >>

```
<p style="color: red; margin-left: 20px">
This is a paragraph. It's colored red and indented 20px.
</p>
```

This is a paragraph. It's colored red and indented 20px.

Figure 20.5

N O T E   Read *Learn CSS with w3schools* to learn more about working with style sheets.

Style Tags

TAG	DESCRIPTION
<style>	Defines a style definition
<link>	Defines a resource reference
<div>	Defines a section in a document
<span>	Defines a section in a document
<font>	Deprecated. Use styles instead
<basefont>	Deprecated. Use styles instead
<center>	Deprecated. Use styles instead

CHAPTER 21

HTML CHARACTER ENTITIES

In This Chapter

❑ Character Entities

❑ Nonbreaking Space

❑ Commonly Used Character Entities

Character Entities

Some characters are reserved in HTML. For example, you cannot use the greater than or less than signs within your text because the browser could mistake them for markup. If you want the browser to actually display these characters, you must insert character entities in the HTML source.

A character entity looks like this: &entity_name; or &#entity_number;

To display a less than sign, you must write: < or <

The advantage of using an entity name instead of a number is that the name often is easier to remember. However, the disadvantage is that browsers may not support all entity names (while the support for entity numbers is very good).

The following example lets you experiment with character entities. The results of the code appear in Figure 21.1.

Try it yourself >>

```
<html>
<body>

<h1>Character Entities</h1>
<p>Code: &X;</p>
<p>
```

(continued)

(continued)

```
    Substitute the "X" with an entity number like "#174" or an
        entity name like "pound" to see the result. Use the table
        in the next section to try different character entities.
    </p>
    <p>&cent;</p>
    <p>&#174;</p>
    <p>&amp;</p>
    </body>
    </html>
```

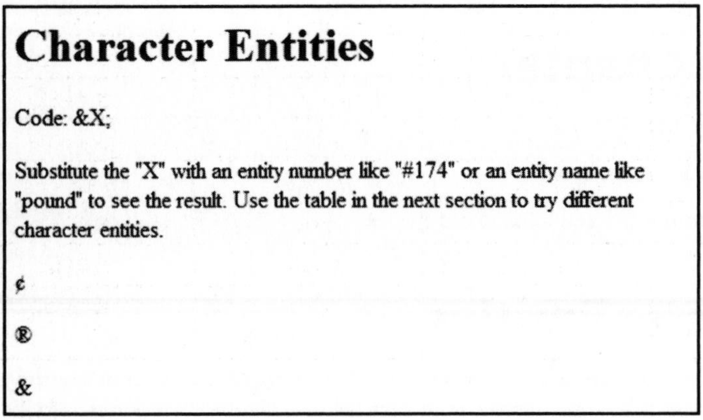

Character Entities

Code: &X;

Substitute the "X" with an entity number like "#174" or an entity name like "pound" to see the result. Use the table in the next section to try different character entities.

¢

®

&

Figure 21.1

Nonbreaking Space

The most common character entity in HTML is the nonbreaking space.

Normally, HTML truncates spaces in your text. If you write 10 spaces in your text, HTML will remove 9 of them. To add lots of spaces to your text, use the   character entity.

Commonly Used Character Entities

> **N O T E**   Entity names are case sensitive!

RESULT	DESCRIPTION	ENTITY NAME	ENTITY NUMBER
	nonbreaking space		
<	less than	&lt;	&#60;
>	greater than	&gt;	&#62;
&	ampersand	&amp;	&#38;
¢	cent	&cent;	&#162;
£	pound	&pound;	&#163;
¥	yen	&yen;	&#165;
€	euro	&euro;	&#8364;
§	section	&sect;	&#167;
©	copyright	&copy;	&#169;
®	registered trademark	&reg;	&#174;

For a complete reference of all character entities, visit the w3schools HTML Entities Reference:

 http://www.w3schools.com/tags/ref_entities.asp

CHAPTER 22

HTML HEAD AND META ELEMENTS

In This Chapter

❑ Head Element

❑ Meta Element

Head Element

The head element **<head>** contains general information, also called meta-information, about a document. Meta means "information about". You can say that meta-data means information about data, or meta-information means information about information. The head element includes important information such as the document's title, style instructions, and more.

What's Inside the Head Element?

According to the HTML standard, only a few tags are legal inside the head section. The legal tags include the following:

▶▶ `<base>`

▶▶ `<title>`

▶▶ `<meta>`

▶▶ `<link>`

▶▶ `<style>`

▶▶ `<script>`

> You learned more about the `<link>` and `<style>` tags in Chapter 20, "HTML CSS Styles."

The elements inside the `<head>` element are not intended to be displayed by a browser. Look at the following illegal construct:

Try it yourself >>

```
<head>
<p>This is some text</p>
</head>
```

In this example, the browser has two options:

▶▶ Display the text because it is inside a `<p>` element.

▶▶ Hide the text because it is inside a `<head>` element.

As Figure 22.1 demonstrates, if you put an HTML element like <h1> or <p> inside a `head` element like this, most browsers will display it, even if it is illegal.

This is some text

Figure 22.1

Should browsers forgive you for errors like this? We don't think so. Others do.

title Tag

The document's title information inside a head element is not displayed in the browser window, but is used for indexing and cataloging. The result of the following code is shown in Figure 22.2.

Try it yourself >>

```
<html>

<head>
<title>The document title is hidden</title>
</head>

<body>
<p>This text is displayed</p>
</body>

</html>
```

This text is displayed

Figure 22.2

151

base Tag

The example illustrated in Figure 22.3 demonstrates how to use the <base> tag to let all the links on a page open in a new window.

Try it yourself >>

```
<html>
<head>
<base target="_blank">
</head>

<body>

<p>
<a href="http://www.w3schools.com"
target="_blank">This link</a>
will load in a new window because the target attribute is
    set to "_blank".
</p>

<p>
<a href="http://www.w3schools.com">
This link</a>
will also load in a new window even without a target attri-
    bute.
</p>

</body>
</html>
```

This link will load in a new window because the target attribute is set to "_blank".

This link will also load in a new window even without a target attribute.

Figure 22.3

Head Tags

TAG	DESCRIPTION
<head>	Defines information about the document
<title>	Defines the document title
<base>	Defines a base URL for all the links on a page
<link>	Defines a resource reference
<meta>	Defines meta information
<!DOCTYPE>	Defines the document type and tells the browser which version of the markup language the page is written in. This tag goes before the <html> start tag.

A full list of legal attributes for each element is listed in the w3schools Complete HTML Reference online at:

 http://www.w3schools.com/tags

Meta Element

As discussed earlier in the last section, the head element contains general information (meta-information) about a document.

HTML also includes a meta element <meta> that goes inside the head element. The purpose of the meta element is to provide meta-information about the document. Most often the meta element is used to provide information that is relevant to browsers or search engines, like describing the content of your document.

The meta attributes in the following example identify the document's author, editor, and the software used to create the page.

```
<html>

<head>

<meta name="author"
content="Jan Egil Refsnes">

<meta name="revised"
content="Michael Woodward,3/14/2010">

<meta name="generator"
```

(continued)

153

(continued)

```
content="Microsoft FrontPage 5.0">

</head>

</html>
```

You can see a complete list of the meta element attributes in the w3schools.com HTML 4.01 Tag Reference:

http://www.w3schools.com/html/html_reference.asp

Keywords for Search Engines

Information inside a meta element can also describe the document's keywords, which are used by search engines to find your page when a user conducts a search on the keyword.

Try it yourself >>

```
<html>

<head>

<meta name="description"
content="HTML examples">

<meta name="keywords"
content="HTML, DHTML, CSS, XML, JavaScript, VBScript">

</head>

<body>
<p>
The meta attributes of this document describe the document
    and its keywords.
</p>
</body>

</html>
```

The intention of the `name` and `content` attributes is to describe the content of a page, such as:

```
<meta name="description" content="Free Web tutorials on
    HTML, CSS, XML, and SML" />
<meta name="keywords" content="HTML, DHTML, CSS, XML,
    JavaScript" />
```

Some search engines on the Web will use the `<name>` and `<content>` attributes of the `meta` tag to index your pages. However, because too many Webmasters have used meta tags for spamming, like repeating keywords to give pages a higher search ranking, some search engines have stopped using them entirely.

You can read more about search engines in the w3schools.com Web Building Tutorial at:

 http://www.w3schools.com/site/

Unknown Meta Attributes

Sometimes you will see `meta` attributes that are unknown to you, such as:

```
<meta name="security" content="low" />
```

Then you just have to accept that this is something unique to the site or to the author of the site, and that it has probably no relevance to you.

Redirect a User

This example demonstrates how to redirect a user if your site address has changed.

Try it yourself >>

```
<html>
<head>
<meta http-equiv="Refresh"
content="5;url=http://www.w3schools.com">
</head>

<body>
<p>
Sorry! We have moved! The new URL is: <a href="http://www.
    w3schools.com">http://www.w3schools.com</a>
</p>
```

(continued)

(continued)

```
<p>
You will be redirected to the new address in five seconds.
</p>

<p>
If you see this message for more than 5 seconds, please
    click on the link above!
</p>

</body>
</html>
```

> **NOTE**   The W3 Consortium states that "Some user agents support the use of META to refresh the current page after a specified number of seconds, with the option of replacing it by a different URL. Authors should not use this technique to forward users to different pages, as this makes the page inaccessible to some users. Instead, automatic page forwarding should be done using server-side redirects." For more information, visit the W3 Web site:
>
> http://www.w3.org/TR/html4/struct/global.html#adef-http-equiv

CHAPTER 23

HTML UNIFORM RESOURCE LOCATORS

In This Chapter

❑ Uniform Resource Locator (URL)

❑ URL Schemes

❑ Using Links

Uniform Resource Locator (URL)

Something called a uniform resource locator (URL) is used to address a document (or other data) on the World Wide Web. When you click on a link in an HTML document, an underlying <a> tag points to a place (an address) on the Web with an href attribute value like this:

```
<a href="lastpage.htm">Last Page</a>
```

The lastpage.htm link in the example is a link that is relative to the Web site that you are browsing, and your browser will construct a full Web address to access the page, such as:

```
http://www.w3schools.com/html/lastpage.htm
```

A full Web address follows these syntax rules:

```
scheme://host.domain:port/path/filename
```

▶▶ The **scheme** is defining the type of Internet service. The most common type is http.

▶▶ The **domain** is defining the Internet domain name like w3schools.com.

▶▶ The **host** is defining the domain host. If omitted, the default host for http is www.

▶▶ The **:port** is defining the port number at the host. The port number is normally omitted. The default port number for http is 80.

157

▸▸ The **path** is defining a path (a subdirectory) at the server. If the path is omitted, the resource (the document) must be located at the root directory of the Web site.

▸▸ The **filename** is defining the name of a document. The default filename might be default.asp, index.html, or something else depending on the settings of the Web server.

URL Schemes

Some examples of the most common schemes can be found in the following table:

SCHEMES	ACCESS
file	a file on your local PC
ftp	a file on an FTP server
http	a file on a World Wide Web Server
gopher	a file on a Gopher server
news	a Usenet newsgroup
telnet	a Telnet connection
WAIS	a file on a WAIS server

Accessing a Newsgroup

The following HTML code:

```
<a href="news:alt.html">HTML Newsgroup</a>
```

creates a link to a newsgroup.

Downloading with FTP

The following HTML code:

```
<a href="ftp://www.w3schools.com/ftp/winzip.exe">Download
  WinZip</a>
```

creates a link to an FTP directory. (The link doesn't work. Don't try it. It's just an example. w3schools doesn't really have an FTP directory.)

Link to your Mail system

The following HTML code:

```
<a href="mailto:someone@w3schools.com">someone@w3schools.
  com</a>
```

creates a link that opens a new e-mail message addressed to the address in the link.

Using Links

The following sample code shows how to use the three types of URL links described. Results of the code appear in Figure 23.1.

Try it yourself >>

```html
<html>
<body>
<p><a href="news:alt.html">HTML Newsgroup</a></p>

<p><a href="ftp://www.w3schools.com/ftp/winzip.exe">Download
  WinZip</a></p>

<p><a href="mailto:someone@w3schools.com">someone@w3schools.
  com</a></p>
</body>
</html>
```

HTML Newsgroup

Download WinZip

someone@w3schools.com

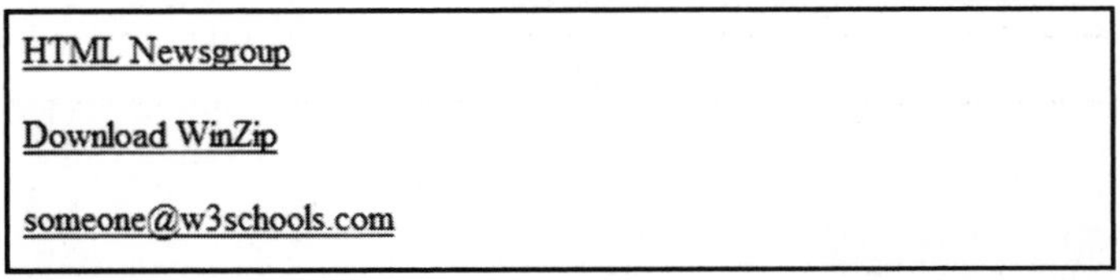

Figure 23.1

CHAPTER 24

HTML SCRIPTS

In This Chapter

- ❏ Insert a Script into a Page
- ❏ How to Handle Older Browsers
- ❏ noscript Tag
- ❏ Script Tags

Insert a Script into a Page

Add scripts to HTML pages to make them more dynamic and interactive. A script in HTML is defined with the <script> tag.

This example demonstrates how to insert a script into your HTML document. Note that you will have to use the **type** attribute to specify the scripting language. The following script produces the output shown in Figure 24.1.

Try it yourself >>

```
<html>
<body>
<script type="text/javascript">
document.write("Hello World!")
</script>

</body>
</html>
```

Hello World!

Figure 24.1

To learn more about scripting in HTML, read w3schools' JavaScript tutorial at:

 http://www.w3schools.com/js/

How to Handle Older Browsers

A browser that does not recognize the `<script>` tag at all will display the `<script>` tag's content as text on the page. To prevent the browser from doing this, you should hide the script in comment tags. An old browser (that does not recognize the `<script>` tag) will ignore the comment, and it will not write the tag's content on the page. On the other hand, a new browser will understand that the script should be executed, even if it is surrounded by comment tags.

```
JavaScript:
<script type="text/javascript">
<!-
document.write("Hello World!")
//-->
</script>


VBScript:
<script type="text/vbscript">
<!-
document.write("Hello World!")
'-->
</script>
```

The following example demonstrates how to prevent browsers that do not support scripting from displaying text unintentionally. The results appear in Figure 24.2.

Try it yourself >>

```
<html>
<body>

<script type="text/javascript">
<!--
document.write("If this is displayed, your browser supports
   scripting!")
//-->
</script>
<noscript>No JavaScript support!</noscript>

</body>
</html>
```

If this is displayed, your browser supports scripting!

Figure 24.2

noscript Tag

In addition to hiding the script inside a comment, you can also add a `<noscript>` tag.

The `<noscript>` tag is used to define an alternate text if a script is NOT executed. This tag is used for browsers that recognize the `<script>` tag, but do not support the script inside, so these browsers will display the text inside the `<noscript>` tag instead. However, if a browser supports the script inside the `<script>` tag it will ignore the `<noscript>` tag.

```
JavaScript:
<script type="text/javascript">
<!--
document.write("Hello World!")
//-->
</script>
<noscript>Your browser does not support JavaScript!</
  noscript>


VBScript:
<script type="text/vbscript">
<!-
document.write("Hello World!")
'-->
</script>
<noscript>Your browser does not support VBScript!</noscript>
```

Script Tags

TAG	DESCRIPTION
<script>	Defines a script
<noscript>	Defines an alternate text if the script is not executed
<object>	Defines an embedded object
<param>	Defines runtime settings (parameters) for an object
<applet>	Deprecated. Use <object> instead

CHAPTER 25

HTML STANDARD ATTRIBUTES

In This Chapter

❏ Core Attributes

❏ Language Attributes

❏ Keyboard Attributes

HTML tags can have attributes. The special attributes for each tag are listed under each tag description. The attributes listed here are the core and language attributes that are standard for all tags (with a few exceptions).

Core Attributes

Not valid in `base`, `head`, `html`, `meta`, `param`, `script`, `style`, and `title` elements.

ATTRIBUTE	VALUE	DESCRIPTION
class	*class_rule or style_rule*	The class of the element
id	*id_name*	A unique id for the element
style	*style_definition*	An inline style definition
title	*tooltip_text*	A text to display in a tool tip

Language Attributes

Not valid in `base`, `br`, `frame`, `frameset`, `hr`, `iframe`, `param`, and `script` elements.

ATTRIBUTE	VALUE	DESCRIPTION
dir	ltr | rtl	Sets the text direction
lang	*language_code*	Sets the language code

Keyboard Attributes

ATTRIBUTE	VALUE	DESCRIPTION
accesskey	*character*	Sets a keyboard shortcut to access an element
tabindex	*number*	Sets the tab order of an element

CHAPTER 26

HTML EVENT ATTRIBUTES

In This Chapter

- ❏ Window Events
- ❏ Form Element Events
- ❏ Keyboard Events
- ❏ Mouse Events

New to HTML 4.0 is the ability to let HTML events trigger actions in the browser, like starting a JavaScript when a user clicks on an HTML element. The following tables list attributes that can be inserted into HTML tags to define event actions.

 If you want to learn more about programming with these events, you should study w3schools' tutorials on JavaScript and DHTML:

JavaScript: http://www.w3schools.com/js

DHTML: http://www.w3schools.com/dhtml

Window Events

These attributes are valid only in **body** and `frameset` elements.

ATTRIBUTE	VALUE	DESCRIPTION
onload	*script*	Script to be run when a document loads
onunload	*script*	Script to be run when a document unloads

Form Element Events

These attributes are valid only in form elements.

ATTRIBUTE	VALUE	DESCRIPTION
onchange	*script*	Script to be run when the element changes
onsubmit	*script*	Script to be run when the form is submitted
onreset	*script*	Script to be run when the form is reset
onselect	*script*	Script to be run when the element is selected
onblur	*script*	Script to be run when the element loses focus
onfocus	*script*	Script to be run when the element gets focus

Keyboard Events

These attributes are not valid in base, bdo, br, frame, frameset, head, html, iframe, meta, param, script, style, and title elements.

ATTRIBUTE	VALUE	DESCRIPTION
onkeydown	*script*	What to do when key is pressed
onkeypress	*script*	What to do when key is pressed and released
onkeyup	*script*	What to do when key is released

Mouse Events

These attributes are not valid in base, bdo, br, frame, frameset, head, html, iframe, meta, param, script, style, and title elements.

ATTRIBUTE	VALUE	DESCRIPTION
onclick	*script*	What to do on a mouse click
ondblclick	*script*	What to do on a mouse double-click
onmousedown	*script*	What to do when mouse button is pressed
onmousemove	*script*	What to do when mouse pointer moves
onmouseout	*script*	What to do when mouse pointer moves out of an element
onmouseover	*script*	What to do when mouse pointer moves over an element
onmouseup	*script*	What to do when mouse button is released

CHAPTER 27

HTML URL ENCODING

In This Chapter

❑ URL Encoding

❑ Common URL Encoding Characters

URL Encoding

URL encoding converts characters into a format that can be safely transmitted over the Internet.

As you learned in Chapter 23, "HTML Uniform Resource Locators," Web browsers request pages from Web servers by using a URL. The URL is the address of a Web page like http://www.w3schools.com.

URLs can only be sent over the Internet using the ASCII character set. ASCII is a 7-bit character set containing 128 characters. It contains the numbers from 0-9, the uppercase and lowercase English letters from A to Z, and some special characters.

 See Appendix G, "HTML ISO-8859-1 Reference," for the complete ASCII character set.

Because URLs often contain characters outside the ASCII set, the URL has to be converted. URL encoding converts the URL into a valid ASCII format. It replaces unsafe ASCII characters with "%" followed by two hexadecimal digits corresponding to the character values in the ISO-8859-1 character set. ISO-8859-1 is the default character set in most browsers.

The first 128 characters of ISO-8859-1 are the original ASCII character set (the numbers from 0-9, the uppercase and lowercase English alphabet, and some special characters). The higher part of ISO-8859-1 (codes from 160-255) contains the characters used in Western European countries and some commonly used special characters.

 See Appendix H, "HTML Symbol Entities Reference" for the complete ISO-8859-1 character set.

URLs cannot contain spaces. URL encoding normally replaces a space with a + sign.

Common URL Encoding Characters

CHARACTER	URL ENCODING
€	%80
£	%A3
©	%A9
®	%AE
À	%C0
Á	%C1
Â	%C2
Ã	%C3
Ä	%C4
Å	%C5
space	%20

 See the w3schools' HTML Language Code Reference for the complete URL Encoding reference.

CHAPTER 28

TURN YOUR PC INTO A WEB SERVER

In This Chapter

Your Windows PC as a Web Server

If you want other people to view your pages, you must publish them. To publish your work, you must save your pages on a Web server.

Your own PC can act as a Web server if you install Internet Information Server (IIS) or Personal Web Server (PWS). IIS or PWS turns your computer into a Web server. Microsoft IIS and PWS are free Web server components.

> **NOTE** Mac OS X users can also run their own local web server simply by checking the "Web Sharing" option in the Systems Sharing preference and then sticking their .html/.css/..Web files in their "Sites" folder. See: http://docs.info.apple.com/article.html?path=Mac/10.6/en/8236.html

Internet Information Server (IIS)

IIS is a set of Internet-based services for servers created by Microsoft for use with Microsoft Windows. IIS comes with Windows 2000, XP, Vista, and 7. It is also available for Windows NT.

IIS is easy to install and ideal for developing and testing Web applications. IIS includes Active Server Pages (ASP), a server-side scripting standard that can be used to create dynamic and interactive Web applications.

If you want to know more about ASP, see the w3schools ASP tutorial:

 http://www.w3schools.com/asp

Personal Web Server (PWS)

PWS is for older Windows systems like Windows 95, 98, and NT. PWS is easy to install and can be used for developing and testing Web applications including ASP.

> **NOTE** We don't recommend running PWS for anything other than training. It is outdated and has security issues.

Windows Web Server Versions

Not all versions of Windows support IIS and/or PWS, but most do. Here's a relatively complete list.

» Windows 7 Home, Professional, Enterprise, and Ultimate come with IIS 7.5

» Windows Vista Business, Enterprise and Ultimate come with IIS 7

» Windows Vista Home Premium comes with IIS 7

» Windows Vista Home Edition does not support PWS or IIS

» Windows XP Professional comes with IIS 5.1

» Windows XP Home Edition does not support IIS or PWS

» Windows 2000 Professional comes with IIS 5.0

» Windows NT Professional comes with IIS 3 and also supports IIS 4

» Windows NT Workstation supports PWS and IIS 3

» Windows Me does not support PWS or IIS

» Windows 98 comes with PWS

» Windows 95 supports PWS

Installing IIS on Windows Vista and Windows 7

Follow these steps to install IIS on Windows Vista or 7:

1. Open the Control Panel from the Start menu.

2. Double-click Programs and Features.

3. Click "Turn Windows features on or off" (a link to the left).

4. Select the check box for Internet Information Services (IIS), and click OK.

After you install IIS, be sure to run Microsoft Update to install all patches for bugs and security problems. Test your Web, as explained later in this chapter.

Installing IIS on Windows XP and Windows 2000

Follow these steps to install IIS on Windows XP and Windows 2000:

1. On the Start menu, click Settings and select Control Panel.

2. Double-click Add or Remove Programs.

3. Click Add/Remove Windows Components.

4. Click Internet Information Services (IIS).

5. Click Details.

6. Select the check box for World Wide Web Service, and click OK.

7. In Windows Component selection, click Next to install IIS.

After you install IIS, be sure to run Microsoft Update to install all patches for bugs and security problems. Test your Web, as described next.

Testing Your Web

After you install IIS or PWS, follow these steps:

1. Look for a new folder called Inetpub on your hard drive.

2. Open the Inetpub folder, and find a folder named wwwroot.

3. Create a new folder under wwwroot and name it something like "MyWeb."

4. Write some ASP code and save the file as test1.asp in the new folder.

5. Make sure your Web server is running.

6. Open your browser and type "http://localhost/MyWeb/test1.asp" to view your first Web page.

> **NOTE** Look for the IIS (or PWS) symbol in your Start menu or taskbar. The program has functions for starting and stopping the Web server, disabling and enabling ASP, and much more.

Installing PWS on Windows 95, 98, and Windows NT

Follow these steps to install PWS on Windows 95, 98, and Windows NT:

▸▸ **Windows 98**. Open the Add-ons folder on your Windows CD, find the PWS folder and double-click runsetup.exe to install PWS.

▸▸ **Windows 95 or Windows NT**. Download Windows NT 4.0 Option Pack from Microsoft, and install PWS.

Test your Web as described earlier.

Your Next Step: A Professional Web Server

If you do not want to use PWS or IIS, you must upload your files to a public server. Most Internet service providers (ISPs) will offer to host your Web pages. If your employer has an Internet server, you can ask him to host your Web site.

If you are really serious about this, you should install your own Internet server. Before you select an ISP, be sure you read w3schools Web Hosting Tutorial at:

 http://www.w3schools.com/hosting

CHAPTER 29

HTML AND CSS SUMMARY

You Have Learned HTML, Now What?

This tutorial has taught you how to use HTML to create your own Web site.

HTML is the universal markup language for the Web. HTML lets you format text, add graphics, create links, input forms, frames, and tables, and so on, and save it all in a text file that any browser can read and display.

The key to HTML is the tags, which indicate what content is coming up.

For more information on HTML, the w3schools.com Web site offers two helpful tools you can study:

 HTML Examples: http://www.w3schools.com/html/html_examples.asp

 HTML Reference: http://www.w3schools.com/tags

What's Next?

The next step is to learn CSS.

CSS

CSS is used to control the style and layout of multiple Web pages all at once. With CSS, all formatting can be removed from the HTML document and stored in a separate file. CSS gives you total control of the layout, without messing up the document content.

 You can learn more about styles and CSS in the companion book *Learn CSS and HTML with w3schools*, or by visiting http://www.w3schools.com/css.

Section III
Appendixes

HTML 4.01 REFERENCE

If you visit this reference on the w3schools Web site, you will find links for each item in the Property column that point to syntax, examples, browser support, and so on:

 http://www.w3schools.com/tags

DTD

This indicates in which HTML 4.01 DTD the tag is allowed. S=Strict, T=Transitional, and F=Frameset.

 For more information about DTDs, see Chapter 19, "Why Use HTML 4.0?"

 For more information about DTDs, visit the w3schools reference HTML <!DOCTYPE> Declaration at http://www.w3schools.com/tags/tag_doctype.asp.

Ordered Alphabetically

TAG	DESCRIPTION	DTD
<!--...-->	Defines a comment	STF
<!DOCTYPE>	Defines the document type	STF
<a>	Defines an anchor	STF
<abbr>	Defines an abbreviation	STF
<acronym>	Defines an acronym	STF
<address>	Defines contact information for the author/owner of a document	STF

TAG	DESCRIPTION	DTD
<applet>	Deprecated. Defines an embedded applet	TF
<area />	Defines an area inside an image-map	STF
<b>	Defines bold text	STF
<base />	Defines a default address or a default target for all links on a page	STF
<basefont />	Deprecated. Defines a default font, color, or size for the text in a page	TF
<bdo>	Defines the text direction	STF
<big>	Defines big text	STF
<blockquote>	Defines a long quotation	STF
<body>	Defines the document's body	STF
 	Defines a single line break	STF
<button>	Defines a pushbutton	STF
<caption>	Defines a table caption	STF
<center>	Deprecated. Defines centered text	TF
<cite>	Defines a citation	STF
<code>	Defines computer code text	STF
<col />	Defines attribute values for one or more columns in a table	STF
<colgroup>	Defines a group of columns in a table for formatting	STF
<dd>	Defines a description of a term in a definition list	STF
<del>	Defines deleted text	STF
<dfn>	Defines a definition term	STF
<dir>	Deprecated. Defines a directory list	TF
<div>	Defines a section in a document	STF
<dl>	Defines a definition list	STF
<dt>	Defines a term (an item) in a definition list	STF
<em>	Defines emphasized text	STF
<fieldset>	Defines a border around elements in a form	STF
<font>	Deprecated. Defines font, color, and size for text	TF
<form>	Defines an HTML form for user input	STF

TAG	DESCRIPTION	DTD
<frame />	Defines a window (a frame) in a frameset	F
<frameset>	Defines a set of frames	F
<h1> to <h6>	Defines HTML headings	STF
<head>	Defines information about the document	STF
<hr />	Defines a horizontal line	STF
<html>	Defines an HTML document	STF
<i>	Defines italic text	STF
<iframe>	Defines an inline frame	TF
<img />	Defines an image	STF
<input />	Defines an input control	STF
<ins>	Defines inserted text	STF
<isindex>	Deprecated. Defines a searchable index related to a document	TF
<kbd>	Defines keyboard text	STF
<label>	Defines a label for an input element	STF
<legend>	Defines a caption for a fieldset element	STF
<li>	Defines a list item	STF
<link />	Defines the relationship between a document and an external resource	STF
<map>	Defines an image-map	STF
<menu>	Deprecated. Defines a menu list	TF
<meta />	Defines metadata about an HTML document	STF
<noframes>	Defines an alternate content for users that do not support frames	TF
<noscript>	Defines an alternate content for users that do not support client-side scripts	STF
<object>	Defines an embedded object	STF
<ol>	Defines an ordered list	STF
<optgroup>	Defines a group of related options in a select list	STF
<option>	Defines an option in a select list	STF
<p>	Defines a paragraph	STF
<param />	Defines a parameter for an object	STF
<pre>	Defines preformatted text	STF

TAG	DESCRIPTION	DTD
<q>	Defines a short quotation	STF
<s>	Deprecated. Defines strikethrough text	TF
<samp>	Defines sample computer code	STF
<script>	Defines a client-side script	STF
<select>	Defines a select list (drop-down list)	STF
<small>	Defines small text	STF
<span>	Defines a section in a document	STF
<strike>	Deprecated. Defines strikethrough text	TF
<strong>	Defines strong text	STF
<style>	Defines style information for a document	STF
<sub>	Defines subscripted text	STF
<sup>	Defines superscripted text	STF
<table>	Defines a table	STF
<tbody>	Groups the body content in a table	STF
<td>	Defines a cell in a table	STF
<textarea>	Defines a multiline text input control	STF
<tfoot>	Groups the footer content in a table	STF
<th>	Defines a header cell in a table	STF
<thead>	Groups the header content in a table	STF
<title>	Defines the title of a document	STF
<tr>	Defines a row in a table	STF
<tt>	Defines teletype text	STF
<u>	Deprecated. Defines underlined text	TF
<ul>	Defines an unordered list	STF
<var>	Defines a variable part of a text	STF
<xmp>	Deprecated. Defines preformatted text	

Ordered by Function

TAG	DESCRIPTION	DTD
Basic		
<!DOCTYPE>	Defines the document type	STF
<html>	Defines an HTML document	STF
<body>	Defines the document's body	STF

TAG	DESCRIPTION	DTD
<h1> to <h6>	Defines HTML headings	STF
<p>	Defines a paragraph	STF
 	Inserts a single line break	STF
<hr />	Defines a horizontal line	STF
<!--...-->	Defines a comment	STF
Formatting		
<acronym>	Defines an acronym	STF
<abbr>	Defines an abbreviation	STF
<address>	Defines contact information for the author/owner of a document	STF
<b>	Defines bold text	STF
<bdo>	Defines the text direction	STF
<big>	Defines big text	STF
<blockquote>	Defines a long quotation	STF
<center>	Deprecated. Defines centered text	TF
<cite>	Defines a citation	STF
<code>	Defines computer code text	STF
<del>	Defines deleted text	STF
<dfn>	Defines a definition term	STF
<em>	Defines emphasized text	STF
<font>	Deprecated. Defines font, color, and size for text	TF
<i>	Defines italic text	STF
<ins>	Defines inserted text	STF
<kbd>	Defines keyboard text	STF
<pre>	Defines preformatted text	STF
<q>	Defines a short quotation	STF
<s>	Deprecated. Defines strikethrough text	TF
<samp>	Defines sample computer code	STF
<small>	Defines small text	STF
<strike>	Deprecated. Defines strikethrough text	TF
<strong>	Defines strong text	STF
<sub>	Defines subscripted text	STF
<sup>	Defines superscripted text	STF
<tt>	Defines teletype text	STF

TAG	DESCRIPTION	DTD
<u>	Deprecated. Defines underlined text	TF
<var>	Defines a variable part of a text	STF
<xmp>	Deprecated. Defines preformatted text	
Forms		
<form>	Defines an HTML form for user input	STF
<input />	Defines an input control	STF
<textarea>	Defines a multiline text input control	STF
<button>	Defines a pushbutton	STF
<select>	Defines a select list (drop-down list)	STF
<optgroup>	Defines a group of related options in a select list	STF
<option>	Defines an option in a select list	STF
<label>	Defines a label for an input element	STF
<fieldset>	Defines a border around elements in a form	STF
<legend>	Defines a caption for a fieldset element	STF
<isindex>	Deprecated. Defines a searchable index related to a document	TF
Frames		
<frame />	Defines a window (a frame) in a frameset	F
<frameset>	Defines a set of frames	F
<noframes>	Defines an alternate content for users that do not support frames	TF
<iframe>	Defines an inline frame	TF
Images		
<img />	Defines an image	STF
<map>	Defines an image-map	STF
<area />	Defines an area inside an image-map	STF
Links		
<a>	Defines an anchor	STF
<link />	Defines the relationship between a document and an external resource	STF
Lists		
<ul>	Defines an unordered list	STF
<ol>	Defines an ordered list	STF

TAG	DESCRIPTION	DTD
<li>	Defines a list item	STF
<dir>	Deprecated. Defines a directory list	TF
<dl>	Defines a definition list	STF
<dt>	Defines a term (an item) in a definition list	STF
<dd>	Defines a description of a term in a definition list	STF
<menu>	Deprecated. Defines a menu list	TF
Tables		
<table>	Defines a table	STF
<caption>	Defines a table caption	STF
<th>	Defines a header cell in a table	STF
<tr>	Defines a row in a table	STF
<td>	Defines a cell in a table	STF
<thead>	Groups the header content in a table	STF
<tbody>	Groups the body content in a table	STF
<tfoot>	Groups the footer content in a table	STF
<col />	Defines attribute values for one or more columns in a table	STF
<colgroup>	Defines a group of columns in a table for formatting	STF
Styles		
<style>	Defines style information for a document	STF
<div>	Defines a section in a document	STF
<span>	Defines a section in a document	STF
Meta Info		
<head>	Defines information about the document	STF
<title>	Defines the document title	STF
<meta>	Defines metadata about an HTML document	STF
<base />	Defines a default address or a default target for all links on a page	STF
<basefont />	Deprecated. Defines a default font, color, or size for the text in a page	TF

TAG	DESCRIPTION	DTD
Programming		
<script>	Defines a client-side script	STF
<noscript>	Defines an alternate content for users that do not support client-side scripts	STF
<applet>	Deprecated. Defines an embedded applet	TF
<object>	Defines an embedded object	STF
<param />	Defines a parameter for an object	STF

HTML STANDARD ATTRIBUTES

The attributes listed in this appendix are standard. They are supported by all HTML and tags with a few exceptions.

If you visit this reference on the w3schools Web site, you will find links for each item in the Attribute column that point to syntax, examples, tips, browser support, and so on:

http://www.w3schools.com/tags/ref_standardattributes.asp

Core Attributes

Not valid in `base`, `head`, `html`, `meta`, `param`, `script`, `style`, and `title` elements

ATTRIBUTE	VALUE	DESCRIPTION
class	classname	Specifies a classname for an element
id	id	Specifies a unique id for an element
style	style_definition	Specifies an inline style for an element
title	text	Specifies extra information about an element

Language Attributes

Not valid in base, br, frame, frameset, hr, iframe, param, and script elements

ATTRIBUTE	VALUE	DESCRIPTION
dir	ltr rtl	Specifies the text direction for the content in an element
lang	language_code	Specifies a language code for the content in an element. Language code reference

 For a complete language code reference, visit the w3schools Web site: http://www.w3schools.com/tags/ref_language_codes.asp

Keyboard Attributes

ATTRIBUTE	VALUE	DESCRIPTION
accesskey	character	Specifies a keyboard shortcut to access an element
tabindex	number	Specifies the tab order of an element

HTML STANDARD EVENT ATTRIBUTES

HTML 4 added the ability to let events trigger actions in a browser, like starting a JavaScript when a user clicks on an element.

 To learn more about programming events, please read *Learn JavaScript and Ajax with w3schools*, also from Wiley Publishing, or visit the JavaScript tutorial at www.w3schools.com/js.

 Also be sure to visit the DHTML tutorial at www.w3schools.com/dhtml

The following tables list the standard event attributes that can be inserted into HTML elements to define event actions.

body and frameset Events

These attributes can only be used in `<body>` or `<frameset>`:

ATTRIBUTE	VALUE	DESCRIPTION
onload	script	Script to be run when a document loads
onunload	script	Script to be run when a document unloads

Form Events

These attributes can be used in `form` elements.

ATTRIBUTE	VALUE	DESCRIPTION
onblur	script	Script to be run when an element loses focus
onchange	script	Script to be run when an element changes
onfocus	script	Script to be run when an element gets focus
onreset	script	Script to be run when a form is reset
onselect	script	Script to be run when an element is selected
onsubmit	script	Script to be run when a form is submitted

187

Image Events

This attribute can be used with the img element.

ATTRIBUTE	VALUE	DESCRIPTION
onabort	script	Script to be run when loading of an image is interrupted

Keyboard Events

Valid in all elements except base, bdo, br, frame, frameset, head, html, iframe, meta, param, script, style, and title.

ATTRIBUTE	VALUE	DESCRIPTION
onkeydown	script	Script to be run when a key is pressed
onkeypress	script	Script to be run when a key is pressed and released
onkeyup	script	Script to be run when a key is released

Mouse Events

Valid in all elements except base, bdo, br, frame, frameset, head, html, iframe, meta, param, script, style, and title.

ATTRIBUTE	VALUE	DESCRIPTION
onclick	script	Script to be run on a mouse click
ondblclick	script	Script to be run on a mouse double-click
onmousedown	script	Script to be run when mouse button is clicked
onmousemove	script	Script to be run when mouse pointer moves
onmouseout	script	Script to be run when mouse pointer moves out of an element
onmouseover	script	Script to be run when mouse pointer moves over an element
onmouseup	script	Script to be run when mouse button is released

HTML ELEMENTS AND VALID DOCTYPES

If you visit this reference on the w3schools Web site, you will find links for each item in the Tag column that point to syntax, examples, tips, browser support, and so on:

www.w3schools.com/tags/tag_doctype.asp

 For more information about DTDs, see Chapter 19, "Why Use HTML 4.0?"

For more information about DTDs, visit the w3schools reference "HTML <!DOC-TYPE> Declaration" at:

www.w3schools.com/tags/tag_doctype.asp.

The following table lists all HTML elements and defines which doctype declarations (DTDs) each element appears in.

TAG	HTML 4.01		
	TRANSITIONAL	STRICT	FRAMESET
<a>	Yes	Yes	Yes
<abbr>	Yes	Yes	Yes
<acronym>	Yes	Yes	Yes
<address>	Yes	Yes	Yes
<applet>	Yes	No	Yes
<area />	Yes	Yes	Yes
<b>	Yes	Yes	Yes
<base />	Yes	Yes	Yes
<basefont />	Yes	No	Yes
<bdo>	Yes	Yes	Yes

TAG	HTML 4.01		
	TRANSITIONAL	STRICT	FRAMESET
<blockquote>	Yes	Yes	Yes
<body>	Yes	Yes	Yes
 	Yes	Yes	Yes
<button>	Yes	Yes	Yes
<caption>	Yes	Yes	Yes
<center>	Yes	No	Yes
<cite>	Yes	Yes	Yes
<code>	Yes	Yes	Yes
<col />	Yes	Yes	Yes
<colgroup>	Yes	Yes	Yes
<dd>	Yes	Yes	Yes
<del>	Yes	Yes	Yes
<dfn>	Yes	Yes	Yes
<dir>	Yes	No	Yes
<div>	Yes	Yes	Yes
<dl>	Yes	Yes	Yes
<dt>	Yes	Yes	Yes
<em>	Yes	Yes	Yes
<fieldset>	Yes	Yes	Yes
<font>	Yes	No	Yes
<form>	Yes	Yes	Yes
<frame />	No	No	Yes
<frameset>	No	No	Yes
<h1> to <h6>	Yes	Yes	Yes
<head>	Yes	Yes	Yes
<hr />	Yes	Yes	Yes
<html>	Yes	Yes	Yes
<i>	Yes	Yes	Yes
<iframe>	Yes	No	Yes
<img />	Yes	Yes	Yes
<input />	Yes	Yes	Yes
<ins>	Yes	Yes	Yes

TAG	HTML 4.01		
	TRANSITIONAL	STRICT	FRAMESET
<kbd>	Yes	Yes	Yes
<label>	Yes	Yes	Yes
<legend>	Yes	Yes	Yes
<li>	Yes	Yes	Yes
<link />	Yes	Yes	Yes
<map>	Yes	Yes	Yes
<menu>	Yes	No	Yes
<meta />	Yes	Yes	Yes
<noframes>	Yes	No	Yes
<noscript>	Yes	Yes	Yes
<object>	Yes	Yes	Yes
<ol>	Yes	Yes	Yes
<optgroup>	Yes	Yes	Yes
<option>	Yes	Yes	Yes
<p>	Yes	Yes	Yes
<param />	Yes	Yes	Yes
<pre>	Yes	Yes	Yes
<q>	Yes	Yes	Yes
<s>	Yes	No	Yes
<samp>	Yes	Yes	Yes
<script>	Yes	Yes	Yes
<select>	Yes	Yes	Yes
<small>	Yes	Yes	Yes
<span>	Yes	Yes	Yes
<strike>	Yes	No	Yes
<strong>	Yes	Yes	Yes
<style>	Yes	Yes	Yes
<sub>	Yes	Yes	Yes
<sup>	Yes	Yes	Yes
<table>	Yes	Yes	Yes
<tbody>	Yes	Yes	Yes
<td>	Yes	Yes	Yes

TAG	HTML 4.01		
	TRANSITIONAL	STRICT	FRAMESET
<tfoot>	Yes	Yes	Yes
<th>	Yes	Yes	Yes
<thead>	Yes	Yes	Yes
<title>	Yes	Yes	Yes
<tr>	Yes	Yes	Yes
<tt>	Yes	Yes	Yes
<u>	Yes	No	Yes
<ul>	Yes	Yes	Yes
<var>	Yes	Yes	Yes

HTML CHARACTER SETS

 For more information about working with character sets, see Chapter 27, "URL Encoding."

ASCII Characters

To display an HTML page correctly, the browser must know what character set to use. The character set for the early World Wide Web was ASCII. ASCII supports the numbers from 0-9, the uppercase and lowercase English alphabet, and some special characters.

 For more about ASCII, see Appendix F, "HTML ASCII Reference."

 A complete list of the ASCII character set is available at www.w3schools. com/tags/ref_ascii.asp.

ISO-8859-1 Characters

Because many countries use characters that are not a part of ASCII, the default character set for modern browsers is ISO-8859-1.

 For more about ISO characters, see Appendix G, "HTML ISO-8859-1 Reference."

 A complete list of the ISO-8859-1 character set is available at www. w3schools.com/tags/ref_entities.asp.

Other ISO Character Sets

It is the International Organization for Standardization (ISO) that defines the standard character sets for different alphabets/languages.

> **TIP** If a Web page uses a different character set than ISO-8859-1, it should be specified in the `<meta>` tag.

The different character sets being used around the world are listed in the following table:

CHARACTER SET	DESCRIPTION	COVERS
ISO-8859-1	Latin alphabet part 1	North America, Western Europe, Latin America, the Caribbean, Canada, Africa
ISO-8859-2	Latin alphabet part 2	Eastern Europe
ISO-8859-3	Latin alphabet part 3	SE Europe, Esperanto, miscellaneous others
ISO-8859-4	Latin alphabet part 4	Scandinavia/Baltics (and others not in ISO-8859-1)
ISO-8859-5	Latin/Cyrillic part 5	The languages that are using a Cyrillic alphabet such as Bulgarian, Belarusian, Russian and Macedonian
ISO-8859-6	Latin/Arabic part 6	The languages that are using the Arabic alphabet
ISO-8859-7	Latin/Greek part 7	The modern Greek language as well as mathematical symbols derived from the Greek
ISO-8859-8	Latin/Hebrew part 8	The languages that are using the Hebrew alphabet
ISO-8859-9	Latin 5 part 9	The Turkish language. Same as ISO-8859-1 except Turkish characters replace Icelandic ones
ISO-8859-10	Latin 6 Lappish, Nordic, Eskimo	The Nordic languages
ISO-8859-15	Latin 9 (aka Latin 0)	Similar to ISO-8859-1 but replaces some less common symbols with the euro sign and some other missing characters

CHARACTER SET	DESCRIPTION	COVERS
ISO-2022-JP	Latin/Japanese part 1	The Japanese language
ISO-2022-JP-2	Latin/Japanese part 2	The Japanese language
ISO-2022-KR	Latin/Korean part 1	The Korean language

Unicode Standard

Because the character sets listed in the preceding table are limited in size and are not compatible in multilingual environments, the Unicode Consortium developed the Unicode Standard. The Consortium's goal is to replace the existing character sets with its standard Unicode Transformation Format (UTF).

The Unicode Standard covers all the characters, punctuations, and symbols in the world. Unicode enables processing, storage, and interchange of text data no matter what the platform, no matter what the program, no matter what the language.

TIP The first 256 characters of Unicode character sets correspond to the 256 characters of ISO-8859-1.

The Unicode Standard has become a success and is implemented in XML, Java, ECMAScript (JavaScript), LDAP, CORBA 3.0, WML, and so on. The Unicode Standard is also supported in many operating systems and all modern browsers. The Unicode Consortium cooperates with the leading standards development organizations, like ISO, W3C, and ECMA.

Unicode can be implemented by different character sets. The most commonly used encodings are UTF-8 and UTF-16 include the following:

CHARACTER SET	DESCRIPTION
UTF-8	A character in UTF-8 can be from 1 to 4 bytes long. UTF-8 can represent any character in the Unicode standard. UTF-8 is backwards compatible with ASCII. UTF-8 is the preferred encoding for e-mail and Web pages.
UTF-16	16-bit Unicode Transformation Format is a variable-length character encoding for Unicode, capable of encoding the entire Unicode repertoire. UTF-16 is used in major operating systems and environments, like Microsoft Windows 2000/XP/2003/Vista/CE and the Java and .NET byte code environments.

NOTE All HTML 4 processors already support UTF-8, and all XML processors support UTF-8 and UTF-16.

HTML ASCII REFERENCE

 For more information about working with character sets, see Chapter 27, "URL Encoding."

ASCII Character Set

The ASCII character set is used to send information between computers on the Internet. ASCII stands for the American Standard Code for Information Interchange. It was designed in the early 1960s as a standard character set for computers and hardware devices like teleprinters and tapedrives.

ASCII is a 7-bit character set containing 128 characters. It contains the numbers from 0-9, the uppercase and lowercase English letters from A to Z, and some special characters. The character sets used in modern computers, HTML, and the Internet are all based on ASCII.

The following table lists the 128 ASCII characters and their equivalent HTML entity codes.

 A complete list of the ASCII character set is also available at www.w3schools.com/tags/ref_ascii.asp.

ASCII Printable Characters

ASCII CHARACTER	HTML ENTITY CODE	DESCRIPTION
	&#32;	space
!	&#33;	exclamation mark
"	&#34;	quotation mark
#	&#35;	number sign
$	&#36;	dollar sign
%	&#37;	percent sign
&	&#38;	ampersand

ASCII CHARACTER	HTML ENTITY CODE	DESCRIPTION
'	&#39;	apostrophe
(	&#40;	left parenthesis
)	&#41;	right parenthesis
*	&#42;	asterisk
+	&#43;	plus sign
,	&#44;	comma
-	&#45;	hyphen
.	&#46;	period
/	&#47;	slash
0	&#48;	digit 0
1	&#49;	digit 1
2	&#50;	digit 2
3	&#51;	digit 3
4	&#52;	digit 4
5	&#53;	digit 5
6	&#54;	digit 6
7	&#55;	digit 7
8	&#56;	digit 8
9	&#57;	digit 9
:	&#58;	colon
;	&#59;	semicolon
<	&#60;	less-than
=	&#61;	equals-to
>	&#62;	greater-than
?	&#63;	question mark
@	&#64;	at sign
A	&#65;	uppercase A
B	&#66;	uppercase B
C	&#67;	uppercase C
D	&#68;	uppercase D
E	&#69;	uppercase E
F	&#70;	uppercase F
G	&#71;	uppercase G
H	&#72;	uppercase H

ASCII CHARACTER	HTML ENTITY CODE	DESCRIPTION
I	&#73;	uppercase I
J	&#74;	uppercase J
K	&#75;	uppercase K
L	&#76;	uppercase L
M	&#77;	uppercase M
N	&#78;	uppercase N
O	&#79;	uppercase O
P	&#80;	uppercase P
Q	&#81;	uppercase Q
R	&#82;	uppercase R
S	&#83;	uppercase S
T	&#84;	uppercase T
U	&#85;	uppercase U
V	&#86;	uppercase V
W	&#87;	uppercase W
X	&#88;	uppercase X
Y	&#89;	uppercase Y
Z	&#90;	uppercase Z
[	&#91;	left square bracket
\	&#92;	backslash
]	&#93;	right square bracket
^	&#94;	caret
_	&#95;	underscore
`	&#96;	grave accent
a	&#97;	lowercase a
b	&#98;	lowercase b
c	&#99;	lowercase c
d	&#100;	lowercase d
e	&#101;	lowercase e
f	&#102;	lowercase f
g	&#103;	lowercase g
h	&#104;	lowercase h
i	&#105;	lowercase i
j	&#106;	lowercase j
k	&#107;	lowercase k

ASCII CHARACTER	HTML ENTITY CODE	DESCRIPTION
l	&#108;	lowercase l
m	&#109;	lowercase m
n	&#110;	lowercase n
o	&#111;	lowercase o
p	&#112;	lowercase p
q	&#113;	lowercase q
r	&#114;	lowercase r
s	&#115;	lowercase s
t	&#116;	lowercase t
u	&#117;	lowercase u
v	&#118;	lowercase v
w	&#119;	lowercase w
x	&#120;	lowercase x
y	&#121;	lowercase y
z	&#122;	lowercase z
{	&#123;	left curly brace
|	|	vertical bar
}	&#125;	right curly brace
~	&#126;	tilde

ASCII Device Control Characters

The ASCII device control characters were originally designed to control hardware devices. Control characters have nothing to do inside an HTML document.

ASCII CHARACTER	HTML ENTITY CODE	DESCRIPTION
NUL	&#00;	null character
SOH	&#01;	start of header
STX	&#02;	start of text
ETX	&#03;	end of text
EOT	&#04;	end of transmission
ENQ	&#05;	enquiry
ACK	&#06;	acknowledge
BEL	&#07;	bell (ring)
BS	&#08;	backspace

ASCII CHARACTER	HTML ENTITY CODE	DESCRIPTION
HT	&#09;	horizontal tab
LF	&#10;	line feed
VT	&#11;	vertical tab
FF	&#12;	form feed
CR	&#13;	carriage return
SO	&#14;	shift out
SI	&#15;	shift in
DLE	&#16;	data link escape
DC1	&#17;	device control 1
DC2	&#18;	device control 2
DC3	&#19;	device control 3
DC4	&#20;	device control 4
NAK	&#21;	negative acknowledge
SYN	&#22;	synchronize
ETB	&#23;	end transmission block
CAN	&#24;	cancel
EM	&#25;	end of medium
SUB	&#26;	substitute
ESC	&#27;	escape
FS	&#28;	file separator
GS	&#29;	group separator
RS	&#30;	record separator
US	&#31;	unit separator
DEL	&#127;	delete (rubout)

HTML ISO-8859-1 REFERENCE

Modern browsers support several character sets:

- ▸▸ ASCII character set (see Appendix F, "HTML ASCII Reference")

- ▸▸ Standard ISO character sets (see Appendix E, "HTML Character Sets")

- ▸▸ Unicode Transformation Format (UTF) (see Appendix E, "HTML Character Sets")

- ▸▸ Mathematical symbols, Greek letters, and other symbols (see Appendix H, "HTML Symbol Entities Reference")

ISO-8859-1

ISO-8859-1 is the default character set in most browsers.

The first 128 characters of ISO-8859-1 make up the original ASCII character set (the numbers from 0-9, the uppercase and lowercase English alphabet, and some special characters).

The higher part of ISO-8859-1 (codes from 160-255) contains the characters used in Western European countries and some commonly used special characters.

Reserved Characters in HTML

Some characters are reserved in HTML. For example, you cannot use the greater-than or less-than signs within your text because the browser could mistake them for markup.

Entities are used to implement reserved characters or to express characters that cannot easily be entered with the keyboard.

HTML processors must support the five special characters listed in the following table.

NOTE	Entity names are case sensitive.

CHARACTER	ENTITY NUMBER	ENTITY NAME	DESCRIPTION
"	"	"	quotation mark
'	'	' (does not work in IE)	apostrophe
&	&	&	ampersand
<	<	<	less-than
>	>	>	greater-than

ISO 8859-1 Symbols

CHARACTER	ENTITY NUMBER	ENTITY NAME	DESCRIPTION
			nonbreaking space
¡	¡	¡	inverted exclamation mark
¢	¢	¢	cent
£	£	£	pound
¤	¤	¤	currency
¥	¥	¥	yen
¦	¦	¦	broken vertical bar
§	§	§	section
¨	¨	¨	spacing diaeresis
©	©	©	copyright
ª	ª	ª	feminine ordinal indicator
«	«	«	angle quotation mark (left)
¬	¬	¬	negation
	­	­	soft hyphen
®	®	®	registered trademark
¯	¯	¯	spacing macron
°	°	°	degree
±	±	±	plus-or-minus

CHARACTER	ENTITY NUMBER	ENTITY NAME	DESCRIPTION
²	&#178;	&sup2;	superscript 2
³	&#179;	&sup3;	superscript 3
´	&#180;	&acute;	spacing acute
µ	&#181;	&micro;	micro
¶	&#182;	&para;	paragraph
·	&#183;	&middot;	middle dot
¸	&#184;	&cedil;	spacing cedilla
¹	&#185;	&sup1;	superscript 1
º	&#186;	&ordm;	masculine ordinal indicator
»	&#187;	&raquo;	angle quotation mark (right)
¼	&#188;	&frac14;	fraction 1/4
½	&#189;	&frac12;	fraction 1/2
¾	&#190;	&frac34;	fraction 3/4
¿	&#191;	&iquest;	inverted question mark
×	&#215;	&times;	multiplication
÷	&#247;	&divide;	division

ISO 8859-1 Characters

CHARACTER	ENTITY NUMBER	ENTITY NAME	DESCRIPTION
À	&#192;	&Agrave;	capital a, grave accent
Á	&#193;	&Aacute;	capital a, acute accent
Â	&#194;	&Acirc;	capital a, circum-flex accent
Ã	&#195;	&Atilde;	capital a, tilde
Ä	&#196;	&Auml;	capital a, umlaut mark
Å	&#197;	&Aring;	capital a, ring
Æ	&#198;	&AElig;	capital ae
Ç	&#199;	&Ccedil;	capital c, cedilla

CHARACTER	ENTITY NUMBER	ENTITY NAME	DESCRIPTION
È	&#200;	&Egrave;	capital e, grave accent
É	&#201;	&Eacute;	capital e, acute accent
Ê	&#202;	&Ecirc;	capital e, circumflex accent
Ë	&#203;	&Euml;	capital e, umlaut mark
Ì	&#204;	&Igrave;	capital i, grave accent
Í	&#205;	&Iacute;	capital i, acute accent
Î	&#206;	&Icirc;	capital i, circumflex accent
Ï	&#207;	&Iuml;	capital i, umlaut mark
Ð	&#208;	&ETH;	capital eth, Icelandic
Ñ	&#209;	&Ntilde;	capital n, tilde
Ò	&#210;	&Ograve;	capital o, grave accent
Ó	&#211;	&Oacute;	capital o, acute accent
Ô	&#212;	&Ocirc;	capital o, circumflex accent
Õ	&#213;	&Otilde;	capital o, tilde
Ö	&#214;	&Ouml;	capital o, umlaut mark
Ø	&#216;	&Oslash;	capital o, slash
Ù	&#217;	&Ugrave;	capital u, grave accent
Ú	&#218;	&Uacute;	capital u, acute accent
Û	&#219;	&Ucirc;	capital u, circumflex accent
Ü	&#220;	&Uuml;	capital u, umlaut mark

CHARACTER	ENTITY NUMBER	ENTITY NAME	DESCRIPTION
Ý	&#221;	&Yacute;	capital y, acute accent
Þ	&#222;	&THORN;	capital THORN, Icelandic
ß	&#223;	&szlig;	small sharp s, German
à	&#224;	&agrave;	small a, grave accent
á	&#225;	&aacute;	small a, acute accent
â	&#226;	&acirc;	small a, circumflex accent
ã	&#227;	&atilde;	small a, tilde
ä	&#228;	&auml;	small a, umlaut mark
å	&#229;	&aring;	small a, ring
æ	&#230;	&aelig;	small ae
ç	&#231;	&ccedil;	small c, cedilla
è	&#232;	&egrave;	small e, grave accent
é	&#233;	&eacute;	small e, acute accent
ê	&#234;	&ecirc;	small e, circumflex accent
ë	&#235;	&euml;	small e, umlaut mark
ì	&#236;	&igrave;	small i, grave accent
í	&#237;	&iacute;	small i, acute accent
î	&#238;	&icirc;	small i, circumflex accent
ï	&#239;	&iuml;	small i, umlaut mark
ð	&#240;	&eth;	small eth, Icelandic
ñ	&#241;	&ntilde;	small n, tilde
ò	&#242;	&ograve;	small o, grave accent

CHARACTER	ENTITY NUMBER	ENTITY NAME	DESCRIPTION
ó	&#243;	&oacute;	small o, acute accent
ô	&#244;	&ocirc;	small o, circumflex accent
õ	&#245;	&otilde;	small o, tilde
ö	&#246;	&ouml;	small o, umlaut mark
ø	&#248;	&oslash;	small o, slash
ù	&#249;	&ugrave;	small u, grave accent
ú	&#250;	&uacute;	small u, acute accent
û	&#251;	&ucirc;	small u, circumflex accent
ü	&#252;	&uuml;	small u, umlaut mark
ý	&#253;	&yacute;	small y, acute accent
þ	&#254;	&thorn;	small thorn, Icelandic
ÿ	&#255;	&yuml;	small y, umlaut mark

HTML SYMBOL ENTITIES REFERENCE

This entity reference includes mathematical symbols, Greek characters, various arrows, technical symbols, and shapes.

NOTE	Entity names are case sensitive.

Math Symbols Supported by HTML

CHARACTER	ENTITY NUMBER	ENTITY NAME	DESCRIPTION
∀	∀	∀	for all
∂	∂	∂	part
∃	∃	&exists;	exists
∅	∅	∅	empty
∇	∇	∇	nabla
∈	∈	∈	isin
∉	∉	∉	notin
∋	∋	∋	ni
∏	∏	∏	prod
∑	∑	∑	sum
−	−	−	minus
∗	∗	∗	lowast
√	√	√	square root
∝	∝	∝	proportional to
∞	∞	∞	infinity
∠	∠	∠	angle

CHARACTER	ENTITY NUMBER	ENTITY NAME	DESCRIPTION
∧	&#8743;	&and;	and
∨	&#8744;	&or;	or
∩	&#8745;	&cap;	cap
∪	&#8746;	&cup;	cup
∫	&#8747;	&int;	integral
∴	&#8756;	&there4;	therefore
~	&#8764;	&sim;	similar to
≅	&#8773;	&cong;	congruent to
≈	&#8776;	&asymp;	almost equal
≠	&#8800;	&ne;	not equal
≡	&#8801;	&equiv;	equivalent
≤	&#8804;	&le;	less or equal
≥	&#8805;	&ge;	greater or equal
⊂	&#8834;	&sub;	subset of
⊃	&#8835;	&sup;	superset of
⊄	&#8836;	&nsub;	not subset of
⊆	&#8838;	&sube;	subset or equal
⊇	&#8839;	&supe;	superset or equal
⊕	&#8853;	&oplus;	circled plus
⊗	&#8855;	&otimes;	circled times
⊥	&#8869;	&perp;	perpendicular
·	&#8901;	&sdot;	dot operator

Greek Letters Supported by HTML

CHARACTER	ENTITY NUMBER	ENTITY NAME	DESCRIPTION
Α	&#913;	&Alpha;	Alpha
Β	&#914;	&Beta;	Beta
Γ	&#915;	&Gamma;	Gamma
Δ	&#916;	&Delta;	Delta
Ε	&#917;	&Epsilon;	Epsilon
Ζ	&#918;	&Zeta;	Zeta

CHARACTER	ENTITY NUMBER	ENTITY NAME	DESCRIPTION
Η	&#919;	&Eta;	Eta
Θ	&#920;	&Theta;	Theta
Ι	&#921;	&Iota;	Iota
Κ	&#922;	&Kappa;	Kappa
Λ	&#923;	&Lambda;	Lambda
Μ	&#924;	&Mu;	Mu
Ν	&#925;	&Nu;	Nu
Ξ	&#926;	&Xi;	Xi
Ο	&#927;	&Omicron;	Omicron
Π	&#928;	&Pi;	Pi
Ρ	&#929;	&Rho;	Rho
	undefined		Sigmaf
Σ	&#931;	&Sigma;	Sigma
Τ	&#932;	&Tau;	Tau
Υ	&#933;	&Upsilon;	Upsilon
Φ	&#934;	&Phi;	Phi
Χ	&#935;	&Chi;	Chi
Ψ	&#936;	&Psi;	Psi
Ω	&#937;	&Omega;	Omega
α	&#945;	&alpha;	alpha
β	&#946;	&beta;	beta
γ	&#947;	&gamma;	gamma
δ	&#948;	&delta;	delta
ε	&#949;	&epsilon;	epsilon
ζ	&#950;	&zeta;	zeta
η	&#951;	&eta;	eta
θ	&#952;	&theta;	theta
ι	&#953;	&iota;	iota
κ	&#954;	&kappa;	kappa
λ	&#955;	&lambda;	lambda
μ	&#956;	&mu;	mu
ν	&#957;	&nu;	nu

CHARACTER	ENTITY NUMBER	ENTITY NAME	DESCRIPTION
ξ	&#958;	&xi;	xi
o	&#959;	&omicron;	omicron
π	&#960;	&pi;	pi
ρ	&#961;	&rho;	rho
ς	&#962;	&sigmaf;	sigmaf
σ	&#963;	&sigma;	sigma
τ	&#964;	&tau;	tau
υ	&#965;	&upsilon;	upsilon
φ	&#966;	&phi;	phi
χ	&#967;	&chi;	chi
ψ	&#968;	&psi;	psi
ω	&#969;	&omega;	omega
ϑ	&#977;	&thetasym;	theta symbol
ϒ	&#978;	&upsih;	upsilon symbol
ϖ	&#982;	&piv;	pi symbol

Other Entities Supported by HTML

CHARACTER	ENTITY NUMBER	ENTITY NAME	DESCRIPTION
Œ	&#338;	&OElig;	capital ligature OE
œ	&#339;	&oelig;	small ligature oe
Š	&#352;	&Scaron;	capital S with caron
š	&#353;	&scaron;	small S with caron
Ÿ	&#376;	&Yuml;	capital Y with diaeres
ƒ	&#402;	&fnof;	f with hook
ˆ	&#710;	&circ;	modifier letter circumflex accent
˜	&#732;	&tilde;	small tilde
			en space
			em space
			thin space
	&#8204;	&zwnj;	zero width non-joiner

CHARACTER	ENTITY NUMBER	ENTITY NAME	DESCRIPTION
	&#8205;	&zwj;	zero width joiner
	&#8206;	&lrm;	left-to-right mark
	&#8207;	&rlm;	right-to-left mark
–	&#8211;	&ndash;	en dash
—	&#8212;	&mdash;	em dash
'	&#8216;	&lsquo;	left single quotation mark
'	&#8217;	&rsquo;	right single quotation mark
‚	&#8218;	&sbquo;	single low-9 quotation mark
"	&#8220;	&ldquo;	left double quotation mark
"	&#8221;	&rdquo;	right double quotation mark
„	&#8222;	&bdquo;	double low-9 quotation mark
†	&#8224;	&dagger;	dagger
‡	&#8225;	&Dagger;	double dagger
•	&#8226;	&bull;	bullet
…	&#8230;	&hellip;	horizontal ellipsis
‰	&#8240;	&permil;	per mille
′	&#8242;	&prime;	minutes
″	&#8243;	&Prime;	seconds
‹	&#8249;	&lsaquo;	single left angle quotation
›	&#8250;	&rsaquo;	single right angle quotation
‾	&#8254;	&oline;	overline
€	&#8364;	&euro;	euro
™	&#8482;	&trade;	trademark
←	&#8592;	&larr;	left arrow
↑	&#8593;	&uarr;	up arrow
→	&#8594;	&rarr;	right arrow
↓	&#8595;	&darr;	down arrow

CHARACTER	ENTITY NUMBER	ENTITY NAME	DESCRIPTION
↔	&#8596;	&harr;	left right arrow
↵	&#8629;	&crarr;	carriage return arrow
⌈	&#8968;	&lceil;	left ceiling
⌉	&#8969;	&rceil;	right ceiling
⌊	&#8970;	&lfloor;	left floor
⌋	&#8971;	&rfloor;	right floor
◊	&#9674;	&loz;	lozenge
♠	&#9824;	&spades;	spade
♣	&#9827;	&clubs;	club
♥	&#9829;	&hearts;	heart
♦	&#9830;	&diams;	diamond

HTML URL ENCODING REFERENCE

URL encoding converts characters into a format that can be safely transmitted over the Internet.

Web browsers request pages from Web servers by using a URL. The URL is the address of a Web page like: http://www.w3schools.com.

 For more information, see Chapter 27, "URL Encoding."

URL Encoding

URLs can only be sent over the Internet using the ASCII character set.

Because URLs often contain characters outside the ASCII set, the URL has to be converted. URL encoding converts the URL into a valid ASCII format. URL encoding replaces unsafe ASCII characters with "%" followed by two hexadecimal digits corresponding to the character values in the ISO-8859-1 character set.

> **NOTE** URLs cannot contain spaces. URL encoding normally replaces a space with a + sign.

 For more about ASCII, see Appendix F, "HTML ASCII Reference."

For more about ISO characters, see Appendix G, "HTML ISO-8859-1 Reference."

URL Encoding Functions

In JavaScript, PHP, and ASP there are functions that can be used to URL encode a string.

In JavaScript you can use the `encodeURI()` function. PHP has the `rawurlencode()` function and ASP has the `Server.URLEncode()` function.

 To learn more about programming events, please read *Learn JavaScript and Ajax with w3schools*, also from Wiley Publishing, or visit the JavaScript tutorial at www.w3schools.com/js.

> **N O T E**   In the following table, some numbers remain unassigned.

URL Encoding Reference

ASCII CHARACTER	URL-ENCODING
space	%20
!	%21
"	%22
#	%23
$	%24
%	%25
&	%26
'	%27
(	%28
)	%29
*	%2A
+	%2B
,	%2C
-	%2D
.	%2E
/	%2F
0	%30
1	%31
2	%32
3	%33

ASCII CHARACTER	URL-ENCODING
4	%34
5	%35
6	%36
7	%37
8	%38
9	%39
:	%3A
;	%3B
<	%3C
=	%3D
>	%3E
?	%3F
@	%40
A	%41
B	%42
C	%43
D	%44
E	%45
F	%46
G	%47
H	%48
I	%49
J	%4A
K	%4B
L	%4C
M	%4D
N	%4E
O	%4F
P	%50
Q	%51
R	%52
S	%53
T	%54
U	%55

ASCII CHARACTER	URL-ENCODING
V	%56
W	%57
X	%58
Y	%59
Z	%5A
[	%5B
\	%5C
]	%5D
^	%5E
_	%5F
`	%60
a	%61
b	%62
c	%63
d	%64
e	%65
f	%66
g	%67
h	%68
i	%69
j	%6A
k	%6B
l	%6C
m	%6D
n	%6E
o	%6F
p	%70
q	%71
r	%72
s	%73
t	%74
u	%75
v	%76
w	%77

ASCII CHARACTER	URL-ENCODING
x	%78
y	%79
z	%7A
{	%7B
|	%7C
}	%7D
~	%7E
	%7F
€	%80
	%81
‚	%82
ƒ	%83
„	%84
…	%85
†	%86
‡	%87
ˆ	%88
‰	%89
Š	%8A
‹	%8B
Œ	%8C
	%8D
Ž	%8E
	%8F
	%90
'	%91
'	%92
"	%93
"	%94
•	%95
–	%96
—	%97
˜	%98
™	%99

ASCII CHARACTER	URL-ENCODING
š	%9A
›	%9B
œ	%9C
	%9D
ž	%9E
Ÿ	%9F
	%A0
¡	%A1
¢	%A2
£	%A3
	%A4
¥	%A5
¦	%A6
§	%A7
¨	%A8
©	%A9
ª	%AA
«	%AB
¬	%AC
	%AD
®	%AE
¯	%AF
°	%B0
±	%B1
²	%B2
³	%B3
´	%B4
µ	%B5
¶	%B6
·	%B7
¸	%B8
¹	%B9
º	%BA
»	%BB

ASCII CHARACTER	URL-ENCODING
¼	%BC
½	%BD
¾	%BE
¿	%BF
À	%C0
Á	%C1
Â	%C2
Ã	%C3
Ä	%C4
Å	%C5
Æ	%C6
Ç	%C7
È	%C8
É	%C9
Ê	%CA
Ë	%CB
Ì	%CC
Í	%CD
Î	%CE
Ï	%CF
Đ	%D0
Ñ	%D1
Ò	%D2
Ó	%D3
Ô	%D4
Õ	%D5
Ö	%D6
	%D7
Ø	%D8
Ù	%D9
Ú	%DA
Û	%DB
Ü	%DC
Ý	%DD

ASCII CHARACTER	URL-ENCODING
Þ	%DE
ß	%DF
à	%E0
á	%E1
â	%E2
ã	%E3
ä	%E4
å	%E5
æ	%E6
ç	%E7
è	%E8
é	%E9
ê	%EA
ë	%EB
ì	%EC
í	%ED
î	%EE
ï	%EF
ð	%F0
ñ	%F1
ò	%F2
ó	%F3
ô	%F4
õ	%F5
ö	%F6
÷	%F7
ø	%F8
ù	%F9
ú	%FA
û	%FB
ü	%FC
ý	%FD
þ	%FE
ÿ	%FF